THE NEW AGE OF SEX EDUCATION:

How To Talk To Your Teen

about Cybersex and Pornography in the Digital Age

Jennifer Weeks

Ph.D. LPC CAADC CSAT-S

Contents

Introduction

Today, children are "digital natives," interacting with technology from almost the moment they were born. They can access information across a variety of interfaces, from their home computers to their phones, iPads and whatever the newest technology permits. This presents a challenge for parents who want to keep their kids safe. The old rules no longer apply and parents are left three steps behind their children.

This book is born out of my clinical work treating sexual addiction in adults. Many of these individuals share stories about being "caught" by a parent when they were looking at pornography or masturbating. Other clients share stories of their parents never talking to them about sex when they were young, while some had parents who may have left a book for them to read. Other parents even pretended that sex didn't exist.

In some cases, a parent's reaction to catching their child looking at pornography or masturbating has created a deep sense of shame for the child about sex, masturbation and pornography. Combining sex, shame and secrets is the perfect recipe to develop sexual dysfunction or addiction later in life. The one thing these clients have in common is their hindsight desire for their parents to have handled the situation better and to have talked to them.

This is ultimately a book about prevention, learning how to help your child avoid future potential sexual addictions and dysfunctions. If you, as a parent, can learn how to talk to your child about sex in this digital age--in an open, healthy and caring way—together we may be able to prevent the next generation of Internet addicts, pornography addicts or sex addicts.

My goal for this book is to provide parents with tools and guidelines for talking to their children about cybersex in a healthy way. This often requires parents to analyze their own feelings of discomfort about sex before they can talk to their child and also to have a working knowledge of their children's online behavior when it comes to cybersex. Given the rapidly changing nature of technology, I am sure that this will be outdated soon enough. It seems as though as soon as parents figure out what their children are doing online, a new cell phone application ("app") is released that becomes popular, leaving the parents to play "catch up". We adults are always behind the curve.

It is my hope that by reading this book, parents will have a better working knowledge of healthy sexuality and cybersex and be able to talk to their children about these issues in an open, non-shaming way. In doing this, we are teaching the younger generations that sex is something that should be talked about and not hidden or cloaked in shame and secrets.

Chapter 1

●●●●●●●●

Too Many Cupcakes.
Why You Need to Read This Book

I am not normally a fan of scare tactics. I don't know that there is any science or data that tells us that those billboards of pictures of methamphetamine addicts actually stop people from using methamphetamine or that the television ads of ex-smokers with serious physical issues actually stop people from smoking. There seems to be something in human nature that can see an image like that and still say, "Nope, not me. That won't happen to me." We tend to be staunchly fixed in a state of denial when it comes to health and safety. Sometimes I think that we just don't like to sit in reality and much prefer our internal fantasy that nothing bad is ever going to happen, no matter what we do or do not do.

As a parent, you need to read this book because there are potentially stark consequences for inaction or denial. When it comes to technology and children, ignorance is *not* bliss. Ignorance is a problem. Lack of communication is a problem and disconnection is a problem. These are all issues that we need to address and I try to touch on all of these topics in this book.

This book is born out of my work with sexual addicts and cybersex offenders. I wrote this book because during the course of my work with clients I get sad. Sometimes I get really, really sad. We have a tradition in our therapy groups: Jail cupcakes. What are jail cupcakes? On the last day of a group therapy session before a client has to turn himself (less frequently, herself) in to jail or federal prison, I go to Whole Foods and get cupcakes for the group. This tradition started many years ago with a client requesting an ice cream cake as his "last meal" in group before he surrendered to Federal prison for five years. The tradition has stuck around and morphed into cupcakes.

I eat too many cupcakes. Not that I don't love a good cupcake, but we eat them far too often. Along with cupcakes comes a great sadness in sending a person I have worked closely with in therapy for sometimes up to four years, to prison. Some of you might ask why I get so sad when a client goes to jail. Haven't they broken a law and don't they deserve to be punished for it? Of course the answer to that is yes. Yes, they have broken a law. Yes, they deserve to serve a punishment. But here is where my sadness comes. Though they have broken a serious law, they are not bad people. Many of my clients are good, wonderful people who were never given the tools or skills that they needed to function successfully in our world. Most of them come from good families. Most of my clients were drawn into illegal sexual behavior due to a combination of addiction, lack of coping skills and a history that primed them to be susceptible to sexual addictions and very bad decision making.

First, I want to tell you some of their stories. If you read closely, there are lessons to be learned from their histories. If we are wise, we will try hard to learn from their mistakes and not suffer the consequences of our children making these mistakes.

Jake

I met Jake after he completed 45 days at an in-patient treatment program for sexual addiction. Jake was 20. He was a bright young man who had been studying at a college out of town before he went to a rehabilitation program. The startling thing about Jake was not his kindness or his honesty. It was the fact that at age 20, he was facing rather serious criminal charges for the possession of child pornography. This smart, kind young man, with his entire future ahead of him, was looking at spending time in Federal prison.

How on earth did this young man get here? Jake comes from a "normal," middle class family, and was born and raised in the suburbs of a major city. His parents are nice people who are educated and employed. He has one sibling. There is no history in this family of sexual abuse or physical abuse. Jake was given nearly every opportunity he wanted, participating in after school activities, traveling, having family vacations, etc. He is smart. He had a goal and was attending a good university to work to achieve that goal. Jake should never have landed in my office and should never have been about to spend time in a Federal prison.

Jake was born and raised in the digital age. He grew up using computers. Given his Generation Y status, it was completely normal for Jake to satisfy his burgeoning sexual curiosity online. He was able to look at online pornography, and the images peaked his interest. There is nothing either wrong or abnormal about this. Looking at online sexual images is pretty normal for a young man of his age and generation.

So what went awry? Some of the ingredients in this problematic stew involved Jake's personality. He is, by nature, somewhat shy and socially anxious. He was not outgoing and gregarious. He was able to make a few very close friends but social situations made him anxious and talking to girls made him even more anxious. He is also of the generation that chatted online. It was so much easier and less anxiety provoking for him to interact with girls online via chat apps or websites than to talk to them in person. Online, he was able to interact and be himself. Online, he was able to be more outgoing than he was in person and online he could talk to girls without the same fears that in- person interactions brought on. The online world was safe. He could get both his relationship needs met (through chat) and his sexual curiosity needs met (through pornography).

The second ingredient in this stew involved Jake's parents. Around the same time that he was starting to immerse himself in the online world and become curious about his sexuality, his parents started to have trouble in their marriage. As his parents' marriage became more chaotic and the focus of their energy, Jake coped with the increased stress, anxiety and uncertainty by spending more time online. Unfortunately for him, no one talked to him about his Internet use or thought it was a problem. Jake became what we call the Lost Child. He was the child who didn't make waves. He didn't do anything to bring any notice on himself. He retreated into his own world to try to manage the stress of the family dynamic. His parents, too consumed with the issues in their marriage, didn't notice what was going on with their son. On the outside he looked fine. He was getting good grades and he was accepted to a good college. On the inside, Jake was becoming more consumed by compulsive pornography use and sexual chatting. He was also looking at sexual images of children. Though those images were of girls his age (when he was still a minor), they were illegal images.

Jake's behavior continued unchecked for several years. He would try to stop on his own and he couldn't. He was too scared to talk to his parents about what was going on. He was stuck. Unfortunately, it was the FBI who ended up getting Jake unstuck. After the FBI came, he went to an in-patient facility and began recovery. Today, he has served his prison sentence, has finished school and is trying to create the best life he can. Unfortunately, that life will be stunted by the fact that he will be on the sex offender registry for the next 15 years and will likely have a very hard time getting a job.

What lessons can be learned from Jake's story? First, parents should never assume that everything is fine with a child who is quiet and not causing overt trouble. The child may be struggling on the inside but fearful of telling parents or ashamed of their behavior. Second, parents need to find a way to look outside of their own issues and their marital issues to really see and connect with their children.

Could all of this have been avoided? I think so. Had there been more open communication, less avoidance and less chaos in the house, Jake might not be in the position he is in today.

Ben

It is not an exaggeration to say that Ben was one of the smartest young men I had ever met in my entire life. Not only was he very intelligent but he was also an extremely talented musician. As with many of my clients who are young men, Ben left my office after his first visit and I wondered, how did this talented young man end up in a position where he is being investigated for the possession and distribution of child pornography? The answer to that question has many layers.

Ben, though extremely smart, also suffered from a rather pronounced case of Attention Deficit Disorder (ADD). When focused on something he cared about, he was brilliant. The rest of the time he was distracted. He had a hard time getting school work done. Ben ended up in several schools to try to address his ADD and did finally land in a school that was able to meet his academic needs.

Why do I bring up his ADD? There are data linking hypersexuality to ADD. However, I bring up Ben's ADD because we know that people who have ADD can hyperfocus (meaning focus on a task to the exclusion of all others) on some tasks. For Ben, his ability to hyperfocus occurred when he played music and when he looked at online pornography. When doing either, he could lose himself in the task for hours on end and lose track of time.

Ben, like many others his age, started looking at pornography online in high school. He did not have many romantic relationships and his focus on music and struggles in school led him to be rather isolated. He had a hard time talking to girls and felt he was always the geeky kid in school. To deal with his loneliness and isolation, he looked at online pornography. The online pornography, along with marijuana, were the main coping mechanisms that got Ben through high school and later, college. His inability to cope with his emotions eventually led Ben to drop out of college where he was attending a very prestigious program.

What was different in Ben's case is that his parents did know that he was looking at pornography online, though they didn't know he was also looking at illegal pornography. Ben recounted one day in therapy session that his mother had found him looking at online pornography once when he was a teen, and she freaked out. He told me that she got so upset that she threw the computer against the wall and told him that if he looked at online pornography again he would no longer be her son.

As we will talk about in later chapters, how a parent reacts to the realization that their son or daughter is watching online pornography can have a huge impact on how the child deals with their sexuality for the rest of their life. In Ben's case, he knew, after one encounter, that he could never go to his mother again with any struggles he was having with online pornography. His mother's reaction reinforced his shame about his behavior and induced him to greater secrecy about his addiction. Ben continued to look at pornography and knew what he was doing was illegal. He didn't think there was anyone he could talk to about his behavior and surely wasn't going to tell his parents.

Ben's case worked out well in that he eventually was not charged with a crime, avoiding prison and a lifetime on the Sex Offender Registry. For some reason, the authorities decided not to prosecute his case. We never found out why. His case is the anomaly and not the norm. Despite his story having a somewhat happy ending (no jail time), there are many lessons to learn from his case as well. Again, parents need to talk to their children on a deeper level and find out about their world. Ben and his parents were so focused on finding an academic fit and academic success that they all dismissed or didn't look into other issues that were there. Social isolation, depression and the intense pressure felt by Ben in a highly competitive music world. Even when school was on track, he was not ok. He was not ok but was getting good grades.

Ben's case shows the importance of how you talk to your child when found looking at online pornography. One short lived moment can create a long term scenario where your child feels ashamed of the behavior and their sexuality. Children can instantly become afraid to talk to you about their issues because when you freak out on them, shame them or judge them, you are no longer a safe haven. If a child is going to share their problems, particularly about sex and sexuality, they need to feel that you are safe to do so with.

I could fill up this entire book with stories about the men who I have worked with who became sex addicts or even sex offenders. These men come from all types of families and have all types of backgrounds. Each and every one of them have a story that we can learn from. Most of these men never had good lessons in sex education. Most of these men found the Internet to be a safe and easy way to escape their problems or to talk to people without so much anxiety. Not one of these men ever thought they would end up pornography addicts and not one of these men thought they would end up being registered sex offenders.

I realize that both of these examples are of young men who were arrested for looking at illegal pornography. By doing this, I do not mean to imply that all young men and women who look at pornography when they are young will end up in this position. I use these two cases as worst case scenarios to illustrate that, for some adolescents, watching pornography can have disastrous consequences. I know that there are many young men and women who watch online pornography who do not become addicted and do not end up in trouble with the law.

As a parent, you need to know what your children are doing online. You need to know how to talk to your children, not only about sex but also about cybersex. You need to know how to talk to your children without your own issues about sex and sexuality getting in the way--and you need to talk to your children about sex before someone else does or they learn about sex and sexuality from pornography and the Internet.

You need to talk to your children about sex and cybersex to help them successfully navigate the digital world they live in, and to help them make decisions about their own sexuality in a non-judgmental and healthy way.

When I talk about child pornography prevention I always end by saying that though it may be uncomfortable talking to your child about sex now, imagine how uncomfortable it will be sitting in a court room watching your child be sentenced for a cybersex crime.

Chapter 2

●●●●●●●●●

What Might My Teen
Be Doing Online?

"What are teens—and my teen--doing online?", changes every day. Each day new websites are developed and new apps are gaining in popularity. These technology changes are not only important for parenting but also frequently gain the attention of big business. This is evidenced by *Forbes* magazine running a story early in 2014 titled: "*Where are teens hanging out in 2014 – Hint It's not on Facebook.*"

While apps, texting, social media and video chat may be the crux of teenage social life, they are also big business. There are two places I often learn about new technology that is being used by teenagers, from the teenagers themselves or from *The Wall Street Journal*.

When I started in this work, I was not at all tech savvy. I knew my way around a computer and the Internet for the basics but not much more than that. Each day in the office was and still is a learning experience. I am frequently learning about new ways people use the Internet for sexual purposes.

So what do you do if you are not an IT professional or a tech junkie? Do you have to learn everything that is out there? You don't need to become a "techie" but you do need to be aware and pay attention. It is critical to pay attention to what your kids are doing on their technology as well as pay attention to what you hear and see in the news.

There are multiple ways that teens can engage in cybersex, and multiple platforms on which they can act out. To name a few, cybersex can be accessed on a computer, laptop, smartphone, iPad, iPod, tablet of any kind, ereader, and video gaming systems. Anything that can access the virtual world can be used for sexual purposes. Cybersex comes in many forms as well, such as Internet pornography, sex chat, sexting, webcam apps, social media, anime and smartphone apps. The more technology your teen has, the more exposure to cybersex is possible.

Most parents are aware of some of the apps and websites that teens are using, but not all. Often, when I talk to parents about their child's behavior online, they acknowledge that some teens may be looking at pornography or sexting, but they are sure their child is not doing so.

The average age of first exposure to online pornography is approximately 11 years old. If children are being exposed to online pornography at that age, odds are that your child has at least accidentally seen pornography online and might be viewing it more than accidentally.

Internet Pornography

Pornography has greatly evolved since the days of People v. Larry Flint, the editor of *Hustler Magazine*. What was once considered scandalous--images of naked women--now is what you might label "vanilla" pornography. In the days before freely available Internet access, kids might have found a *Playboy* or *Penthouse* magazine that belonged to a family member or some older neighborhood boy. Today, pornography is as easy to access as anything else online and often, kids come across pornography online even when they are not looking for it. Pornography is a **multibillion** dollar industry with new sites coming online every day. The most prevalent apps for tablets and smartphones are pornography or related to cybersex.

Covenant Eyes, an online filtering and blocking software company, provides statistics about pornography usage on their website. They cite 10 facts about online pornography from an article published in 2008 that will be shocking to most parents.

- *93% of boys and 62% of girls will have exposure to Internet pornography by the time they are 19 years old.*

- *70% of boys have spent at least 30 consecutive minutes online looking at pornography and 35% of those boys have done so more than once.*

- *23% of girls have spent more than 30 consecutive minutes online looking at pornography and 14% have done so more than once.*

Another aspect of today's access to pornography is not just that it is so accessible to children and teens; it is what they are being exposed to that is potentially troublesome. The next chapter will discuss the possible problems this type of exposure can cause in teens. The same article also provides the following facts about what type of pornography children are exposed to.

- *Group Sex – 83% of boys and 57% of girls have seen group sex on the Internet*

- *Same Sex Intercourse – 69% of boys and 55% of girls have seen same sex pornography*

- *Bondage – 39% of boys and 23% of girls have seen pornography that portrays bondage.*

- *Bestiality – 32% of boys and 18% of girls have seen pornography that portrays bestiality.*

- *Sexual Violence – 18% of boys and 10% of girls have seen sexually violent pornography*

- *Child Pornography – 15% of boys and 9% of girls have seen pornography of minors or children engaging in sexual acts.*

Today, it is obvious that children's exposure to pornography can be varied and they are often exposed, sometimes for the first time, to pornography that is difficult for them to understand. In listing these statistics, I am not implying there is inherently anything wrong with the non-illegal types of pornography. My goal is not to demonize pornography or sexuality. My point is that if a child views this pornography, they will likely have a biological reaction to the videos that their minds do not understand. They are also very unlikely to come forward and talk to parents about viewing bestiality or bondage, etc. The key for parents is awareness. We are not in Kansas anymore and things that once were thought of as very outside of the box or taboo are no longer always considered to be so taboo. Additionally, children today are being exposed to much more varied and "hard core" types of pornography than children who grew up in the age of slow dial up connections or who grew up in the pre-Internet age.

So where and how are kids getting access to the Internet? The answer to this question is that they are getting access anywhere there is an Internet, cell or Wi-Fi connection.

Are you aware that there are pornography apps for tablets and cell phones? Most game systems have Internet capability, as do iPods or other mp3 players. They are also gaining access in the old fashioned way, on the laptop or PC. Unlike when the Internet first came into being, most pornography sites today are free. They will ask for some verification of the user being over the age of 18; however, this is done by clicking a box or providing a date of birth. No website actually verifies that the user is at least 18 years old. There are also a large number of sites dedicated to amateur pornography where users can upload their own videos for the world to view. This becomes an additional issue if you have a child who is creating videos of themselves to send to boyfriends or girlfriends. This will be discussed in much more detail later in the book.

SOCIAL MEDIA

FACEBOOK

Facebook is the first name that most people think of when they think about social media. Facebook has been the preeminent player in social media in the post Myspace world. However, by the end of 2013 (Forbes) the number of teens using Facebook started to decline rapidly. Between the first and third quarter of 2013, there was a 16% decrease in usage of Facebook by American teens. So why are kids moving away from Facebook?

The main answer is because of you parents. As more parents and even grandparents become and stay active on Facebook, the less attractive it becomes to teenagers. They do not want to be posting and interacting with friends in a manner that mom or dad or even grandma can see. They are looking for privacy, and having a large number of family members on Facebook doesn't allow for that privacy. You are watching and that is not what they want!

With that being said, there are still a large number of teens using Facebook. It is not only used for posting pictures and in boxing friends, there is also a Facebook messenger app that is popular. Being on Facebook as a parent and being "friends" with your child can be a good way to stay involved with your child's life. However, your children can and do limit the content that you can access or see. Facebook is also home to games that can be played with others throughout the world and offers chat interactions as well as status updates.

Recently, Facebook has introduced Friend Finder to the service. This is a geolocating feature that will allow users to be notified when they are near friends. The app has to be selected by the Facebook user so it will not automatically be activated on Facebook. The app will not display an exact location but will alert the user that a friend is within a half mile radius. It does allow for a Facebook user to disclose an exact location but this is another setting that the user must turn on and it will only display the location for an hour.

Facebook has employed some safeguards in this app to ensure that it is not used for predatory purposes. The user must be 18 years of age or older to use Friend Locator. Additionally, the user has to opt in to the app and therefore will be using it knowingly. The app will be slowly unveiled so that immediate use may not be available for many Facebook users.

So where are kids going now instead of using Facebook? Messaging and Pictures. The data show that the trend in teen use is moving toward messaging apps and image apps such as Flickr. Names you may or may not be familiar with are: Twitter, WhatsApp, Vine, WeChat, Instagram, Snapchat, Keek, and Kik . These are the apps that teens are moving toward using more frequently. As technology moves quickly, these apps and sites will likely soon be outdated and teens will move on to new apps.

TWITTER

Twitter is one of the standard social media names. Most people know about Twitter and Tweeting. According to the company website, there are 241 million active monthly users and 500 million tweets are sent per day. According to MediaBistro, 22% of teenagers use Twitter. When using Twitter, the user can tweet either text only or text and photographs. Most tweets are to the general public but users have the ability to tweet privately to other users. Misunderstandings of this medium can be seen in public scandals such as that of Anthony Weiner, who infamously tweeted a risqué picture of himself out to the twitter universe. It can be assumed he thought that tweet was going to a single person.

For teens, the number of followers on twitter and other such apps can be seen as measures of popularity. It can also be a means for social bullying and isolation.

One teen I worked with provides a good example of this social effect. The tweets that were going around in her social circle were not overt bullying. However, the posts about who was doing what with whom socially, had the effect of ostracizing some people from the school and had large social implications and also had a large impact on the stress, anxiety and mental health of my client.

TUMBLR

Tumblr is a social media blogging platform that 61% of teens are using. According to the Tumblr website, it is a social network that allows the user to post photos, text, quotes, links, music or video. This can be done form any smartphone, tablet or traditional computer. The site states that there are 179.5 million blogs with 82.1 million posts. This company was started in 2007. According to the company guidelines, the site is not to be used for: malicious speech, harming minors, glorifying self-harm, "gore, mutilation, bestiality or necrophilia", unflagged NSFW (not safe for work) images, sexually explicit video, harassment along with many other concerns. Though the site guidelines state that sexually explicit video is prohibited, one can find sexually explicit photograms on the site.

VINE

Vine is a video messaging app. It provides opportunity for video and text communication. Again, like other social networking apps, the company does post guidelines for use. It is not to be used for, among other things, pornography and sexually explicit content, or violence and threats.

INSTAGRAM

Instagram is another photo app that allows the user to take a video or picture, customize it with different looks and then share it on Facebook, Twitter or Tumblr. The idea behind the company was to allow mobile phone picture takers to produce more professional looking photographs. According to Mediabistro, 21% of teens are using Instagram. However, the number of teens using Instagram is likely much higher today as this data is a few years old.

FLICKR

Flickr is another online photo sharing app. According to the company, the goals are to help people make their photos available to family and friends and to enable organization and management of photos. As with Instagram, the goal of the app is benign. The community guidelines for the site do list what not to do. Their Don't Forget the Children guideline suggests that if you are going to post a photo or video that you would hesitate to show a child, you should set your content filter setting appropriately. The company asks that nudity not be shown in the buddy icon. Nowhere in the guidelines are there specific guidelines about pornography. Again, though most people who are using this site are doing so in a safe manner, many people are posting illicit images on the site and the content of some of the images might not be appropriate for children.

SNAPCHAT

Snapchat is an app that has been making headlines lately. Its main selling point is the fact that the video or pictures sent between users disappear, after a user specified amount of time, once viewed and therefore reduces the risk of messages being found by others, be that a parent, husband, wife, etc. The reality is that Snapchat was recently hacked and millions of images that were supposed to have been deleted were, in fact, available after the hack. Mediabistro reported 13% of teens are using Snapchat. According to Connectsafely.org, Snapchat is referred to as the "the sexting app". There are many other apps now on the market that are competing with Snapchat and offer the same type of services. These include apps such as Bolt, TapTalk and Mirage. As with all other apps, new ones arrive on the scene frequently that are all some tiny variation of what is already out there. In the time since the first draft of this book was written, SnapChat has gained immense popularity, not just among teens but also among business and celebrities.

KIK

Kik (www.kik.com) is a messenger app that is the first smartphone messenger to have a built in browser that allows users to talk, and browse while sharing with friends. It is available for all smartphone applications. It can also be used on any i-technology such as an iPad or an iPod touch. According to the company website, there are over 100 million users of this chatting app.

One of the advantages of this messaging app that teens like is the ability to do more than just chat. The app allows them to send pictures or video. As always, there are some downfalls. There is no age verification for the app, though that does not always stop someone younger from using the app. Another potential disadvantage is that there are no parental controls on the app.

This app is often used in combination with other apps such as Instagram, which can allow people that your child does not know to send them a message (if they publicize their user name). This fact, along with the lack of parental controls and no age requirement, does open the app up for use for sexual purposes. The app has a 17+ rating and a reputation for being inundated with sexually explicit materials.

I subscribe to Google daily newsfeeds. If you are unfamiliar with this, if you enter certain keywords into the option, each day Google sends you an email with the top headlines from all over the world with your key word. One of the key words I get an email about is sexting. For some time now, in the Google daily email are a large number of Craig's List ads for sexting partners. Most of these requests involve the use of the messaging app, Kik.

YIK YAK

This spring, the app, Yik Yak began to receive a large amount of attention in the news, none of it positive. School officials from Chicago to Georgia have worked to try to ban the app due to its use as a means to cyberbully students.

Yik Yak is a social media app that allows a user to post anonymous messages online. It is an app that utilizes geolocation as users can see comments by those within a five-mile radius of them. It was initially designed for use by college students to use to spread the word about what was happening on college campuses. Technically, no one under the age of 17 is supposed to use the app but as with most or all apps, this is truly unenforceable. The app has become very popular with high school students and has become a problem.

The fact that the app is seen by those close to the user makes it a great venue for bullying. If a user is in a school, the poster could be making comments all the other users in the school are going to see the comments. As we have all seen in the media over the years, cyberbullying can have dangerous consequences with teens, in some cases taking their own lives due to the bullying.

The use of Yik Yak as a cyberbullying venue is a story that actually has a pretty good ending. The reason is that the creators of the app are concerned about who is using it and how it is being used. The company has implemented what they call "geo-fences" around middle schools and high schools. This allows the company to block the use of the app around the school. Users who are on the app despite its 17+ rating now cannot use the app while they are at school. Though this does not solve the problem of cyberbullying using the app, it drastically reduces the opportunities. All schools in the country are not yet mapped within the fence, but the company is working on it. The company has also changed the rating to 17+ which enables parents to block the app if they are using parental controls on their child's device.

WHISPER

Whisper is an anonymous app that fundamentally does the same thing as its non-digital predecessor, Post Secret. This app allows people to anonymously post a secret, desire or simple statement to be seen by all other users. It also notifies users of posts created within a mile of the user. The fundamental difference is that we are now in the digital world and apps are interactive. Whisper then allows users to respond to the posts either publicly or privately. The company has recently implemented some changes that allow users to connect with others with similar interests, which they feel will help them reach an older audience. Most users of Whisper are under the age of 22.

The concept of Whisper seems harmless. It actually could be cathartic for a person to share a secret they have held for perhaps their entire life. The ability to release a little bit of the shame surrounding the secret can be beneficial for the person with the secret. Imagine the relief of being able to get something off your chest that you have held onto for a lifetime!

Yet sometimes it seems like everything in the digital realm also has a downside. Though Whisper can be used to help users purge their secrets, it can also be used to connect with others. This connection can be simple chatting with an anonymous stranger or something a bit more personal or sexual. Whisper is another app that is often used in conjunction with Kik.

MEERKAT AND MEERKAT ROULETTE

The newest addition to this list arrived in early 2015. Meerkat and Meerkat Roulette are both live streaming video apps. When this app first arrived, it was tied entirely to twitter. The app allows the user to live stream anything to the user's twitter followers. The live broadcast triggered a tweet on twitter with the link that people could click on to watch the live stream video. Though there are other apps that do the same thing, for some reason Meerkat became the "darling" of the industry and became a bit of an overnight success story. Not long after the success, twitter shut down the app's access to the site and some thought that would be the end of the app. In fact, this was not what happened. Now users just have to follow people in Meerkat directly instead of using twitter followers.

Meerkat then introduced Meerkat Roulette which bloggers such as TechCrunch called the Chatroullette for Meerkat. This version of the app allows, via the web, a person to go online and see things that are being live streamed throughout the world. You don't have to have the app to do this. If you do this via the Web, a video comes up on your screen with a next button. You just hit next and have no idea what is coming up next. My initial fear with this app is that it would be used as Chatroulette is often used, for sexual purposes. If you go on Chatroulette, you are likely to come across other users who are doing sexual things online.

I have been on Meerkat Roulette several times to check out the new technology. I have yet to see anything on the site that was inappropriate. From my brief visits, it appears as though a lot of what is being live streamed has to do with business meetings, music performances or webinars. Chatroulette is a private chat between two people. Meerkat Roulette is a public chat. It is my hope that the public nature of Meerkat Roulette will keep most of its content out of the x rated realm and perhaps only the truly exhibitionistic might use the app for sexual purposes.

PERISCOPE

In addition to Meerkat, other live streaming apps have followed. Twitter responded with its own live streaming app called Periscope. Though, for the most part, this app is used for business purposes, a few minutes spent on the app quickly show you that anyone can and will live stream anything. This is another app that has the possibility to be used for great things but also for sexual purposes.

YOUNOW

The final live streaming app to talk about at the time of this writing is an app called YouNow. Like the others, this is an app that allows the user to simply stream a video of whatever is going on in their lives. While much of it is inane silliness on the Internet, I have seen a few things that, given my line of work, give me pause. The first time I went on this site to check it out, there were multiple streams of young (what looked like minor) girls simply sleeping. These users of YouNow simply left their phone next to their bed and it filmed and streamed their entire period of sleep. To a digital immigrant, this may just seem like a foreign thing to do, but we were not raised in the instant digital world with few boundaries. It may seem innocuous. Though I abhor fear mongering, I also know that there are people in the world that have various fetishes and some of those fetishes might include arousal to sleeping people and fantasies about sex with sleeping people. While this is fine among consenting adults, if a minor child is live streaming sleep or other behaviors, they may unknowingly become part of this process.

APPS THAT HIDE

Where there is a will there is a way. This is something often heard in our office. When we are dealing with trying to limit a child's access to sexual content in the digital world or trying to create barriers for accountability for someone with a sexual addiction, we must always remember this!

This is particularly true when dealing with parental controls and teens. As soon as a parent installs some sort of parental control or filtering software, many a teen is online looking at YouTube to try to figure out how to uninstall the filter or get around it. Trust me, within minutes, the fix is found on YouTube with detailed instructions. No matter how hard we try, it is nearly impossible to stay one step ahead of the tech savvy digital native! The world of apps offers an array of ways to get around parental intervention.

HIKE

Hike is an app that is gaining popularity in non-American markets. Why is Hike becoming so popular? It is an app that allows its users to send traditional messages for free. It also has other features that teens like such as stickers and emoticons. You can also send voice messages and files such as PDF, Doc, and PPT etc. Though these features are nice, they are not what make the app so attractive to teens. The attraction lies in the privacy settings.

The privacy features allow the user to limit who can see their profile picture. The description on the company website states "say goodbye to stalkers. From the milk man to your aunts to that creepy guy in college…" Only those people who you want to see you will see you. Additionally, another popular feature is the Hidden mode. This allows the user to hide chats and access them only with a password.

A teen featured in an article in Bloomberg (http://www.bloomberg.com/news/2014-08-26/indian-teens-flirt-in-private-as-hike-app-tops-20-million-users.html) stated that he used the app because his parents were always looking over his shoulder at what he was doing on his phone. With the app, he could keep his relationship a secret from his parents. The business world thinks that this feature, the hidden feature, is what will move Hike past apps such as WhatsApp and Facebook Messenger. Hike provides a level of privacy that other messaging apps do not provide. The company actively markets the app to young people living at home. Currently, Hike is not prevalent in the US market, but is starting to be used more in overseas markets. It is possible that this app or one like it will gain users in the US.

POOF

Poof, and other apps like it, is designed to hide your applications from anyone looking at your phone who is not you. The app can do this by hiding the icon altogether or changing the icon of the original app to poof so that the real name is hidden. In the context of parent-child interactions, this app would allow a child to hide what apps they might be using and still claim to be in compliance with a family transparency policy.

WEBCAM SITES

Webcam sites are sites that are based on real time video transmission whether from a laptop webcam, cell phone, or tablet. While these websites can provide some harmless fun, they are often an outlet for exhibitionism and sexual acts online.

CHATROULETTE

Chatroulette is a site where users can interact with new people via text-chat, web-chat or a microphone. According to the company, there are between 3,000 and 30,000 people signed on at any given time. The website states that it discourages use by individuals under the age of 18 and also prohibits "pornographic" behavior. However, Chatroulette has a reputation for having inappropriate content on the site, particularly pornography or exhibitionism. As a result of its poor reputation, the company is working to change the culture of the site by changing its terms of use and creating an algorithm to filter out obscene content. Despite the fact that this filters out about 60% of the inappropriate content, your chances of logging on and seeing someone masturbating on the camera are still rather high.

My favorite story involving this site comes from a sex offender conference. I was in a training session with Dr. David Delmonico, a psychologist who often trains about cybersex issues. His talks tend to have a bit of shock and awe in them. He always pulls up the site he is talking about in his presentation. I have seen him do this twice, both times with the same result. He goes onto Chatroulette and, invariably, within seconds, there appears the webfeed of a masturbating man. This always draws a reaction from the audience, which I never understand, as the audience is often therapists who work with sex offenders or sex addicts!

Last month, I encountered a forensic case in which the client was exposed to child pornography on ChatRoulette. He reported that there are users who, instead of showing what they are doing, show their screen during a session and on the screen, they show movies of child pornography. Though I knew that there was a lot of in person inappropriate sexual behavior that occurred on ChatRoulette, I was unaware of this new form of being exposed to child pornography.

OMEGLE

Omegle is another Internet web chat service that picks another person who is signed on at random for the user to chat with. You have a one-to-one chat, and your identity is anonymous. The site reports that no one under the age of 13 should use the site and that if the user is under 18 the parent or guardian should know about the use. The guidelines also prohibit the transmission of nudity as well as harassment. Again, this is a site where some people are truly just chatting with others around the world but others are exposing themselves, engaging in sex chat or other behaviors inappropriate for minors.

YOUTUBE

YouTube started out as a simple video sharing website and has morphed into a force of its own. It now has over 1 billion users. Today, YouTube is a source not only of informational videos but has many of its own channels and has created its own stars. YouTube can provide helpful information on how to solve a homework problem you can't figure out. It can help you get to the next level on the video game you are currently obsessed with. YouTube can help you figure out how to get around the filter or parental block your parents put on the computer.

YouTube does offer a safety feature to help the user block inappropriate content. As it admits, no filter is 100% perfect. Often, they rely on other users to flag content as inappropriate. Therefore, adult content does slip through the cracks. In addition to adult content on YouTube, there is a lot of content that is not necessarily pornographic but is obviously created for sexual gratification.

ANIME/MANGA

Anime or manga are Japanese cartoons that date back to the 7th century. These cartoons feature very colorful and stylized characters that are often created to look young with big round eyes. Though most manga is non-sexual, some of the cartoons can be pornographic or violent in nature. Anime pornography is also often called Hentai. Recently, manga pornography was in the news in Japan as it was excluded from child pornography possession laws. (http://www.cnn.com/2014/06/18/world/asia/japan-manga-anime-pornography/).

Animated or cartoon pornography can be of adults or children. Often, the characters have very bright colored hair and are depicted with very large genitalia. Anything and everything that can happen in live human pornography can happen in hentai as well as some things that perhaps cannot. For people who grew up on gaming and manga, crossing over into anime pornography might be seen as an easy transition.

What Is Sexting?

Sexting can be defined as sending sexually charged material via any digital means. This can take several forms. First, sexting can occur through text messaging or any other messaging application. Traditionally, this can be flirty texts that escalate into overt sexual content. Sexting can also include taking, sending or receiving photographs or videos that are sexual in nature.

For example, your child might send flirty text messages back and forth with a person he or she is dating. These messages could escalate from simple flirtation to more sexual suggestions. It can then escalate into overtly sexually provocative messages. This appears to be part of courtship in adolescents who have been raised in the digital age and will be discussed further in a later chapter. The form of sexting that garners the most media coverage is that of sending or receiving naked pictures via text messaging, messaging app or other social media. This is a behavior that can occur in the context of a committed relationship between the teens. Often these images are not shared with anyone other than the intended receiver. However, the risk is that, if and when the relationship goes bad, the sexual images cannot be taken back. Once they have been sent, they are out in the universe. If the relationship goes sour, the possessor of the sexual images can, and sometimes does, forward these images to friends or other kids at the school. What was once the providence of a relationship is now public record and public fodder. There are also websites that are labeled revenge pornography websites where people can post sexual images of ex-partners or sexual videos of ex-partners for public consumption.

This behavior enters very sticky territory when we are dealing with sexting minors and images. Depending on the state, a minor can face very serious criminal charges for sexting. Each state has different laws, some of which are designed to minimize the lifelong damage that can come from getting caught sexting. In some states, a minor who has sent a nude picture of self and/or the minor that received the picture can be charged with manufacture (for the person who sent the picture) of child pornography, possession of child pornography and possibly the distribution of child pornography. Some states make this a lesser crime that will not require lifelong sex offender registration. Even if sexting is part of the new norm of adolescent behavior, parents and teens need to be wary as the behavior can have devastating lifelong consequences.

Trying to make an exhaustive list of what teens are doing in the digital realm is an effort in futility. As soon as the words are written on the page, things change. Every day new apps are coming out and teens are migrating to new messaging apps. There is no way that the above listing is the definitive guide to what your adolescents are doing online. However, it does serve as an entry into the world for parents. The best thing that parents can do is to be aware. Read the newspaper or tech blogs and websites. Talk to your children about what the latest trends for apps or websites are among their age group. They are going to like to talk about it. In this way, you are not only showing interest in their world but you are educating yourself in the process.

The only limit to how the digital world can be used for sexuality is one's imagination. If you can think about it there is likely an app or website for whatever your imagining might be.

Chapter 3

●●●●●●●●

The Effect of Cybersex
on Adolescents

Though the media may portray and perhaps you as a parent may think that all use of digital sexual material by adolescents is detrimental, in reality there is a lot of good that can come from having anonymous access to large quantities of material on sexual education. Young people tend to learn about sex from a number of venues. You may have given your child the "birds and the bees" talk and had a sit down conversation about sex. However, many parents do not have this talk with their children due to embarrassment, shame, their own discomfort with sex or other reasons.

Children can gain knowledge from sex education classes at school. However, the quality, depth and accuracy of that education can vary depending on the school district. Children can also learn about sex from their peers. This is not always the best way to garner information. Sex education from peers can be skewed depending on where the peer education came from. Another mode of gaining sexual education is via the media. This can be through videos, movies, TV shows, you tube videos or sexual education websites on the Internet.

For a child who does not get any information regarding sex and sexuality from the parent or caregiver, the Internet can be a wonderful resource. It is also a great way for a child to search out answers to questions about sex or sexuality that they are, perhaps, too embarrassed to ask about. If on a reputable site, the child can gain access to any and all information they need and answer any question they have regarding sex. Another great use for digital sexual media is for education about sexual health and STDs. This is another area where a youth might be too embarrassed to ask a caregiver about, or feel that it is too awkward to talk about, even with peers.

Children who struggle with their sexuality are traditionally not likely to discuss this with their parents. This is another area where digital media can be extremely helpful. The Internet can provide helpful information about questions relating to gender identity and sexual identity. Not only does the Internet provide information, but the digital world can also provide these teens with a social support network. They can find forums, chat rooms or other online arenas where they can talk about their struggles or confusion in an open manner without fear of judgment. For many of these teens, this is the only outlet they have for open discussion about their sexuality.

SEXTING AND ADOLESCENT SEXUAL DEVELOPMENT

Why Do Teens Sext?

I have written before about the generations that are digital natives – "Gen Y". These generations have been brought up using technology as a means of communication. It makes sense then that digital technology will also be used as a means of sexual expression in these generations. All adolescents, regardless of generation, engage in sexual exploration and find ways to express their sexuality. This is a "normal" part of development and sexual development. Sexting, instead of being a criminal behavior in this context, is an extension of the traditional forms of sexual exploration. This is a mobile, digital generation so their sexual exploration is likely to be mobile and digital as well.

Academics Hasinoff (University of Colorado), Boyd (principle researcher at Microsoft Research) and Ling have researched sexting in the context of adolescent socialization. Ling describes adolescence as a time of social emancipation. Teens develop new skills they will use throughout their lives. These skills include learning how to manage and deal with money, developing their own sense of style and integrity, learning how to deal with social institutions and how to navigate personal relationships. They also learn how to deal with their own sexuality and sex. As all teens will and do test boundaries, mobile communication is now the primary means by which teens expand these behaviors. Ling's research suggests an association between mobile phone use and drinking, trouble at school and sexual activity, supporting the idea that today's teens test boundaries in the digital realm.

Ling also suggests that the cell phone plays a huge role in the emancipation process by providing teens with autonomy and flexibility. By having their own phone, they can exert their own influence among their peers and navigate the sexual area of their peers. Texting and sexting fall under this veil of autonomy. Texting allows teens to engage in their social affairs without their parents' knowledge. There is no ability to overhear a phone conversation with a text and parents are not present for much of their children's social interactions, as so much of this occurs via text or social media.

A recent study published in *Mobile Media & Communication* sought to empirically address the reasons why teens sext. To do this, they analyzed the data from the 2010 Pew Internet and American Life study on "Teens and Mobile Phones." The researchers wanted to learn if teens sext as a part of the emancipation process from family.

The results of the study indicated that there was only one significant predictor of whether or not a teen engaged in sexting--and that was age. Older teens were more likely to sext than younger teens. Teens that were heavier texters were more likely to sext as well. This frequent use of the cell phone to connect, particularly with peers, predicted both sending and receiving text messages. The authors find this to be evidence that teens use sexting as part of the process of social and sexual exploration and creation of sexual identity. Consensual sexting among teens is a social practice and not child pornography (despite its legal classification as such).

What Are Teens Sexting?

Based on recent media portrayals, it seems there is a sexting epidemic. Nearly daily, I see another news story of teens being caught sexting. Depending on where the teens live, this can have serious legal ramifications that might last a lifetime. Though this appears to be an everyday occurrence, what we know from the scientific data is just emerging. The research and what the data tell us about sexting is very different from how the media is portraying the behavior among teens.

Just how prevalent is the behavior?

Recent scientific studies put the prevalence of teen sexting at about 10.2%. That means almost 90% of teens from these studies are not sexting.

Other studies have resulted in slightly higher percentages of teens sexting. One study showed that 11.96% of teens surveyed had sent a sext with a photograph. Another study of American teens put the prevalence of sexting at 19%. These teens had sent a nude or semi-nude photo or video of themselves to someone else. The country in which a teen lives also seems to influence whether or not they will sext. European countries show teen sexting rates of between 1% and 5% for boys and between 1% and 4 % for girls. The noted exceptions are the countries of The Czech Republic and Sweden which have sexting rates for both boys and girls over 10%.

Taken together, the current data show us that, unlike the media portrayals of rampant and epidemic teen sexting, roughly 10% of teens engage in sexting. As technology continues to expand, it is likely that these rates will increase. So, for example, your daughter is a high school freshman and has 325 kids in her freshman class. At the low end, 17 of these kids have sent or received a sext and at the high end, 64 of these kids have sexted. Though the numbers aren't high, there is a chance that your teen is one of the 5-29%, or knows someone who is engaging in the behavior.

Your teen's age may also be a predictor of whether or not he or she is sexting. Older teens are more likely to send or receive sexts than younger teens. The type of sexual texts is different as well, depending on age. Younger adolescents might send sexual texts that are created as more of a joke or innuendo than as sexual content. As teens get older the content becomes more sexual.

This makes sense since older teens are more likely to be experimenting with their sexuality with other people.

Teens who are rampant texters are also more likely to be sexters as well. Studies have shown that the more frequently a teen texts, the more likely they are to engage in sexting. This also makes intuitive sense. If your teen's main means of communicating with others is via text, it is a logical assumption that courtships will take place via text as well.

In my youth, we wrote notes that were passed around in class. The content couldn't be too risqué as there was always the chance that the note would get confiscated by the teacher or read by another student. We normally didn't want to risk the exposure or embarrassment. Today, if you use an app like Snapchat, there is little worry about someone other than the intended seeing the message. Sending a sext via traditional text messaging is still risky as they can both be kept by the receiver and spread around as well. We will talk more about sexting and the law later in the book.

Relationship between Sexting and Risk

When it comes to sexting, oneof the big concerns in our academic community involves the risk involved. The basic question is: Are kids who sext more likely to engage in other high risk behaviors.? The concern is not just about high risk sexual behaviors but also about drug and alcohol use and other impulsive risky acts. What is high risk sex for a teen? Unprotected sex. Multiple sex partners. Sexual behavior under the influence of alcohol or other drugs. These behaviors are considered high risk because they put the teens at risk for sexually transmitted diseases, teen pregnancy and non-consensual sex.

Some studies have found that teens who engage in sexting are more likely to have multiple sex partners in a three-month period of time. These teens were also more likely to have unprotected sex. Additionally, the teens in these studies were more likely to engage in alcohol and drug use. These studies are hard to interpret. It ends up being the chicken or the egg argument. Are kids who already engage in high risk behavior, like drugs and alcohol more likely to engage in high risk online sexual activity? Or is it the sexting that makes them prone to other high risk behaviors such as unprotected sex? Honestly, at this point, we don't know.

We do know that there is also a correlation between impulsivity or risk taking and sexting as well. It could be that adolescents who are more prone to be risk takers engage in sexting because there is a sense of risk in the behavior as well. For some teens, sexting could be an impulsive act as well. If I am texting or chatting with someone and they ask for a sexual image, the impulse may be to comply and reply with a sexy image. For those teens who are more impulsive, there is not going to be a mental brake system on board that might make them say, "OK, wait a minute here" and think of the potential consequences.

Teens' Perception of Sexting

Some research studies have looked at sexting from the point of view of the adolescents themselves. Adolescents, parents, and law enforcement all seem to have very different views on sexting. The law sees the behavior as illegal in many instances. Parents often approach the behavior with fear and anxiety. Teens, however, don't think that it is a big deal. For many adolescents, sexting is part of the courtship ritual when forming a new relationship or part of the glue that holds a relationship together. Teens who are in relationships are more likely to sext with their partner than teens who are not in a relationship.

There is a huge amount of media coverage when teens get caught up in a sexting scandal or get caught with potential legal action to follow (more discussion about this later). The concern over getting caught is not something that teens really worry about. In one study, 41% of teens indicated that they thought sexting was "no big deal." What does concern teens about sexting are the peer consequences. Sexting has a very different impact on you based on whether you are a boy or a girl. Sexting is not a gender neutral behavior. So what exactly does that mean?

If you are a boy who sexts or can get a girl to send you a sexy or naked picture, this raises your social status in the peer group. Though much sexting does occur in the context of relationships, this social philosophy stands. Young men who receive sexy pictures can be seen by their peers as the guy who can get the girl, or at least the picture of the girl. Fundamentally, among those adolescents that sext, being a male means that the behavior is seen in a more positive light.

On the other side of the coin are the social perceptions of girls who sext. Many young girls who sext or know girls who sext feel that there is a sexual double standard. They often feel pressured to send a sext or a sexy picture to a boy but if they do, they run the risk of being labeled as slutty. These girls also reported that they often feel pressure to send the pictures to the boys who are requesting them. Fundamentally, girls are judged more harshly by their peers for sexting. The ironic thing about this judgment is that studies show that the boys are the ones making harsher judgments about the girls.

So the cycle goes on. According to teen accounts of sexting, as part of the courtship rituals of digital adolescents, boys ask girls for sexts. The girls report feeling pressure to send the images. This pressure may be real from the boys or perceived pressure to conform to a social norm. If the girl complies and sends the sext, she runs the risk of being labeled a slut both by her female peers as well as male peers and the boy can get a boost to his social standing. This cycle can also explain the concern about consequences for teens. Teens are not worried about the legal consequences but the social consequences. They fear that the images they send might end up in the hands of someone other than the person they were intended for. These images tend to either get shown to some friends of the receiver or distributed, often after the relationship ends (see revenge porn). Teens who sext also fear what damage this may do to their reputation.

Online Pornography and Adolescent Sexual Development

Teens or pre-teens have been exposed to pornography long before the days of the Internet. When I talk to clients, many of them tell stories of finding a *Playboy* or *Penthouse* magazine when they were between the ages of 11 and 14 to15 years old. These magazines were often the property of Dad, another family member, the family member of a friend or were found somewhere in the world. I have had several clients who, as children, found pornography magazines in the woods. Someone had clearly thrown them away in a place that they thought either no one would find or no one would be able to identify the owner. Kids perhaps came across a pornography video collection that Dad or someone else had stashed somewhere in the house. Again, these videos were often what I call "vanilla" pornography or videos that displayed, at some level, more traditional sex and did not venture into the realm of kink or fetishes. When I ask my younger clients about their first exposure to pornography, the majority of them tell me that they first viewed pornography online. Many of them did not intentionally seek out the videos or images but clicked on a pop up or inadvertently ended up on a site with pornography.

If adolescents have been sneaking a peak at pornography as long as there has been pornography, why is exposure to online pornography any different? The difference between today's early access to pornography and the exposure 30 or 40 years ago is all related to technology.

The digital world provides three things to the user: Access, Affordability and Anonymity.

Access and Opportunity

First the digital world greatly increases access and opportunity. In the pre-digital eras, most adolescents found print pornography that someone didn't hide so well or left out accidentally. Though this was not uncommon, it did not happen with great frequency. The amount of material the teen had available when finding pornography in this was often limited. Most teens couldn't or wouldn't buy pornography so had to rely on what was found or perhaps supplied by an older sibling. In early digital days, pornography access became much easier. All a person had to do was google a sexually suggestive word and tons of sites would appear. Often this happened by accident based on how pornography sites use key words. What hampered access in early digital times was download speeds. Even if an adult or teen wanted to download pornography, time was often against them. Images took a long time to download and videos took even longer. Many a person who might have wanted to view pornography likely gave up or ran out of time.

Access today is unlimited. Gone are the days when online access was limited to a desktop computer or even a laptop. You can access these websites from your phone, tablet, ereader device, gaming console or any other device that is hooked up to wifi. When access is so easy, exposure is easy as well. Now that there is high speed cable and other high speed connectivity, users no longer have to wait long for downloads. They are right at your fingertips in an instant. Since access has increased, gotten mobile and more affordable, opportunity increases as well. Many children have access to a cell phone. Many schools are providing tablets for all students to use in their learning process. The United States government wants to make Internet access for all citizens a priority. Though these things all have great upsides, the ease of access to pornography is a downside for parents hoping their teens will avoid watching pornography.

Affordability parallels access. When computers first came out they were big, bulky and expensive. When laptops first came out they were expensive as well. The first Smartphones were also not very affordable. As the price of technology decreases, tablets and smartphones are placed in the hands of more and more users. Possession of high tech gadgets was once the pervue of the wealthy. Today, many men, women and children of all socioeconomic status have a smartphone. Affordability increases access.

Anonymity

The last A is anonymity. The digital world provides an anonymity that the in-person world does not. Again, prior to the availability of digital sexuality, a person had to go to a store to buy a pornographic video or magazine in person. You had to get the magazine either from the back room or the back row of the magazine rack, take it to the cashier and hand them the money. Many of my clients have told me that this was a deterrent for them and decreased their pornography buying. The advent of the Internet completely took away the deterrent. Now, when you are watching pornography from the comfort of your home no one knows what you are doing. You no longer have to purchase pornography. You no longer have to look anyone in the face when purchasing pornography. It is all one simple click away. These three factors, all inherent in the digital world, create a different environment for today's adolescents that increase the likelihood of early exposure and also increase the availability of pornography for continued access.

Types of Pornography and How They May Affect Your Teen

Another difference between pornography exposure today and pornography exposure 30 years ago is reflected in the type of pornography to which adolescents are exposed. Again, in the pre-digital age, most exposure was to print or video content that could be referred to as vanilla. Most content was not very hard core. The most common magazines commonly displayed images of naked women or of sex acts with a heterosexual base and not involving fetishes, but not in an extremely graphic nature. The most extreme type of magazine many of my older clients report finding was *Hustler* magazine. The content of this magazine many years ago was considered a bit more graphic but nothing by today's digital pornography standards. Occasionally a young man might have been exposed to European pornography which I have been told was a bit more graphic than that found in the United States at the time.

With the increased access and availability of all types of pornography in the digital age, childrens' first exposure to pornography is often not something of the "vanilla" nature. As the data from the earlier chapter pointed out, today's children are being exposed to more varied types of pornography and images of a much more graphic nature.

Imagine yourself as an unsuspecting eleven-year-old boy who is working on a homework assignment for school. He enters a search term into Google or Bing to help him with his homework. He clicks on a link and, instead of the topic he was looking for, is a video of a woman performing sex acts on a dog. Or perhaps he sees a video of coercive sex or something that is even more violent? The biology of this eleven-year-old boy will be paying close attention to these videos. They are exciting, disturbing, surely forbidden and likely very confusing. Though the biology of an eleven-year-old may want to pay attention to these images, the brain of this child does not know what to make of the videos. Likely this boy is not going to his parent(s) about what he found online. He is likely to sit on the secret, potentially internalizing shame about having a reaction to images that are likely to be perceived as "bad" by a child like himself.

The level of taboo, kink or violence depicted in these videos is likely going to increase the cognitive confusion about sexual images in general. Research that we will discuss in more depth later, suggests that the images or videos that these teens are watching can actually influence their arousal templates.

While the picture from the research is incomplete, it suggests that if a child's first exposure to online pornography is to Bondage, Discipline, Sadism, Masochism (BDSM), and they continue to watch this type of pornography, they might be hard wiring their arousal template to BDSM themes. Later in life, they may need this type of sexual interaction to become aroused. The exposure to online pornography could be creating arousal templates that might not have developed if the child was not exposed to online pornography.

Most research looking at the effects of online pornography on adolescents focuses on what happens behaviorally when they view pornography. One study conducted by Patricia Greenfield Ph.D. examined inadvertent exposure to online pornography. In her study, she discussed the differences in reaction based on the child's age. Children age 12 or younger who inadvertently view pornography tend to react with several emotions. They may be embarrassed. They may be fearful of being caught or they may feel guilt or confusion. Children who are a little older (13 or older) do not have these same emotional reactions or have them as strongly as the younger children.

When we are talking about the effects of online pornography on children, we really need to distinguish between frequent users of online pornography and non-frequent users. We really cannot demonize all use of pornography by adolescents as viewing pornography is truly an age-appropriate behavior that, for some adolescents, is part of their curiosity about sex. It is truly a normative behavior. However, as with most things, viewing pornography infrequently does not affect people the same way that frequent consumption does.

What is frequent use? As with most scientific studies, most researchers define frequent differently. Some studies describe frequent use as daily pornography use and other studies define frequent as something slightly less than daily. Regardless of how frequent is defined, there does appear to be differences in the effect of pornography based on frequency of use.

In a 2011 study of Swedish male adolescents, the authors Svedin et. al. defined frequent pornography use as daily use and they found that there were significantly more boys in the frequent user group than girls. They also found that, more often than not, the boys in the frequent user group did not live with both parents. These Swedish teenage pornography users had very positive and liberal attitudes about pornography. These boys also reported using drugs and alcohol more than the boys in the non-frequent pornography viewing group.

For the boys in this study, there was a difference between frequent and non-frequent users of pornography in terms of their sexual behavior as well. The boys who frequently viewed pornography in this study had their first sexual encounter before the age of 15 more often than the non-frequent users and reported a level of sexual desire five times greater than the non-frequent viewing boys. Finally, sexually coercive behavior was more than three times more common among the boys that were frequent users of pornography.

This study is illustrative of many of the studies that have been conducted to ascertain the effects of viewing pornography on adolescents. Each study, due to the methods or the study population, all have slightly different findings. In general, the effects of pornography viewing can be broken down into several categories which we will discuss further. What is the impact of pornography on sexual attitudes and beliefs? Is there a relationship between pornography use and sexual behavior? Does viewing pornography have an effect on sexual aggression? How does viewing pornography impact adolescents body image and self esteem? Later, we will also discuss the role of Internet pornography on pornography induced erectile dysfunction.

Let's first look at the impact of viewing online pornography on the attitudes and beliefs about sex and sexuality. Some research studies have shown that the more an adolescent looks at pornography the more likely it is that they will espouse sexually permissive attitudes. The more frequently a teen watches pornography, the more positive they will feel about pornography in general. Frequent users do not see anything wrong with pornography use and can view it as normal and appropriate. Again, the point of this book is not to demonize pornography or sexuality. However, the depiction of sex in pornography often does not mimic what happens in real life and this frequent use affects other attitudes about sex.

Other studies have found that frequent pornography use reinforces the acceptance of traditional gender roles. Particularly, the idea that men are to be in a position of power and the women are to be subservient. The content of much of the heterosexual pornography available online (excluding BDSM themes) portrays the man in the position of power and the woman there as a receptacle for his sexual needs or desires. This portrayal of sexual interactions between heterosexual men and women is likely in contrast to what actually happens in in-person heterosexual sex. If the teen, both boy and girl, espouse these attitudes, sexual expression can become about a power differential as opposed to being an expression of connection and intimacy.

Frequently watching pornography also influences a teen's level of objectifying women. The more sexually explicit material a teen watched online, the more they objectified women. The surprising fact here, for me, is that both the boys and girls would objectify women more. There are no gender differences here. This means that girls who watch pornography also objectify women more than those girls who don't. They are objectifying their own gender and perhaps even themselves. Does this then, perhaps, teach them that their value is in their sexuality and attractiveness instead of in their personality, intelligence, kindness?

There does appear to be a relationship between pornography use and sexual behavior. Studies have shown that those youths who are frequent watchers of pornography begin having sex at an earlier age than those youths who are not frequent watchers of pornography. Teens who are watching pornography are trying out what they see in the videos. A study of Swedish youth showed that 70% of the teens in the study who frequently viewed pornography wanted to try to engage in the sex acts that they had seen in the videos. Only 42% of the boys in the non-frequent user category wanted to try these acts. The thought here is that watching a lot of sexual imagery online desensitizes the youth to the sex acts. They are exciting to watch online and this then translates into actually engaging in the behaviors. This is not necessarily a bad thing, depending on what they are watching, but can lead to risky behavior such as unprotected anal sex or perhaps coercion.

When it comes to the effect of pornography consumption by teens on violence or sexual violence, the data is limited. Most research on pornography and sexual aggression comes from the sex offender field and we really cannot translate that data to adolescents. Data from the Swedish study did point to some effect of frequent pornography use on coercion. They found that frequent consumers of pornography were three times more likely to engage in sexually coercive behavior. We can't really take the limited data from one study and make any definitive statements. This is an area where more research is needed. There might be an effect of watching violent or rape pornography on real life behavior but at this point, we just don't know. Frequent pornography use desensitizes the users to sexual behavior. We could assume that frequent watching of pornography with violent or coercive themes could influence the occurrence of this behavior but at this point it is simply an assumption with little data to back it up.

Not all impacts of watching pornography are directly related to sex itself. Studies have shown that frequent viewing of pornography does have an impact on the self esteem of both boys and girls. The actors in commercially produced pornography often do not look like the rest of the people in the world. Many actors and actresses are physically enhanced through plastic surgery. They are also chosen for the profession based on their physical attributes or the attributes of their sex organs. These facts can have detrimental effects on the young people watching the films. Young women who frequently view pornography see the actresses in pornography as the "ideal" woman. Since their bodies likely fall short of what they see in the movies, they often have a negative self image about their body. Very few natural bodies can compare to those that are created to be the "optimal" sexual being for pornography.

Boys take a self esteem hit in another manner. Boys who frequently watch pornography can have self esteem issues about sexual performance. Again, the male actors in pornography do not depict what happens in real life. These are movies. They are done in multiple takes. The male actors have fluffers who help them maintain an erection during the filming process. Again, if a boy thinks this is "normal" sex, he is likely always going to fall short of what he sees in the movie. It takes a team of people to make a pornography video. When the young man is having sex with his partner, there is no team. It is just real life sex and real life sex is normally not depicted in commercial pornography. If his expectation is to have "porn sex" he will likely never meet his expectation and perhaps think his sexual performance is sub-par. This can be a great hit to his self esteem.

Another area of concern for youth who are frequent consumers of sexually explicit material online is sexual compulsivity. Other terms for this can be pornography addiction or sexual addiction. There is a great controversy about the classification of pornography consumption to be an addiction. I, as a Certified Sexual Addiction Therapist, obviously believe that pornography addiction is a real thing. The dynamic of the clients we are seeing in our practices is also changing. When I first started in this field, most of my clients were older men. As time goes by, the age of clients keeps getting younger and younger. Now, we do encounter young men and women who are in their early teens (and sometimes earlier) who are addicted to online pornography. Aside from my obvious bias that this pornography addiction exists, let's see what the research says.

Studies have shown that the more frequently a teen watches pornography, the more often they will think about sex. These teens also report that their interest in sex increased with the amount of pornography they consumed and there were times when they were often distracted by thoughts about sex. Other studies have shown that, in boys, pornography may be used in a compulsive way in order to deal with emotional distress or uncomfortable feelings. A study of youth in Hong Kong showed that greater consumption of online sexual material was associated with a greater preoccupation with sexual desires and fantasies. Again, in this area, there is limited research and a lot of controversy. As the generations of young people who grew up on digital devices are studied more, it is my belief that we will start to have the scientific research to support what therapists are seeing in their offices.

There is one proviso to all of the information and research on pornography consumption in adolescents. Much of the data that shows the above mentioned effects are from Western Cultures such as the United States or European countries. There seems to be a difference in pornography consumption in other cultures. Again, we are limited by what cultures have been studied scientifically. For example, a 2013 study of youth in Hong Kong showed levels of exposure to online pornography that were much lower than the levels that are reported in research using Western cultures.

Youth Produced Sexual Imagery

In my clinical practice, I work with cybersex offenders. In doing this work, I have had to go to the Federal Customs House in Philadelphia to view the images of child pornography that were on my client's computers. First, let me say that this is something that I dread doing. Viewing these images is horrible. It rocks my entire day and the images stay in my brain for much longer than I want them to. I find the entire process rather distasteful and am glad that I only rarely have to do this.

Why am I bringing this up in a book about online pornography and teens? The fact is that some of the images I have seen on my client's computers were images of teens that were generated by the teens themselves. These images are what we call youth produced sexual imagery. Some of these images may be images or videos that young people were coerced into creating. However, it is clear that some of the images of youth online were voluntarily created. A study that came out in March 2015 indicates that it is mandatory that we talk about the sexual imagery that is produced by the youth themselves. This study was produced by the Internet Watch Foundation in conjunction with Microsoft and was published on March 10, 2015. Over the course of three months, the authors sourced youth produced sexually explicit content from the Internet. During this time, they found 3,803 images and videos that met the criteria for age and youth production. The study produced some startling findings. The study found that 17.5% of the sexual images or videos were of children 15 years of age or younger. 85.9% of this imagery of children under 15 was created using a webcam and almost all of the images were of girls (93.1%).

The study also looked at what types of images were found online. The images were broken down based on a category system used by United Kingdom law enforcement, and are broken down into A, B. and C. Category C images involve no sexual activity with a predominant focus on the naked genitalia of the individuals depicted. Category B images are those that involve non-penetrative sexual activity and Category A involves images that depict penetrative sexual activity, sadism or bestiality. For those children under the age of 15 who are creating sexual content, most (72.4%) are creating category C images. 44.8% of children under 15 are making sexual imagery that is Category B which involves non-penetrative sexual activity and only 2.1% are creating the most severe Category A images. When the study authors looked particularly at the data from images from children 15 or younger, they found even more disturbing information. Images were then broken down into smaller age categories: 7-10, 11-13 and 14-15. Though only 17.5% of the images found in the study time frame were youth produced, the shocking data emerged that 40.3% of the youth produced sexual imagery was produced by children aged 7 to 10 years old. When the Internet Watch Foundation conducted this study in 2012, only three years prior, they had found no images or videos of children under 13 that were self-produced.

The authors of the study stated that there appeared to be several types of imagery. Some of the videos and content were clearly forced or coerced. The children in some of these videos were showing signs of distress and it was hypothesized that they were being blackmailed into performing sexual acts on the webcam. It is not uncommon for child abusers to use sexual images sent by the child as blackmail to induce them to engage in other sexual behaviors.

Often the children will do so as the threat of being exposed either socially or to parents induces them to comply. Though there were sexual images that were clearly coerced, there were also images in this young age category that appeared to be voluntarily produced as well, perhaps for attention on webcam or other social sites. The majority of these images appeared to have been filmed on a webcam that was located in the privacy of the child's bedroom.

Another finding in this study, which is not terribly surprising, is that the images were circulated around the Internet. Though an image or video may have been sent to one particular person or occurred in chat with one particular person, they tended to be harvested from the original websites and posted on third party sites. There was also evidence that some of the images were screen shots of webcam interactions or videos of what the interaction on the computer made with another device.

Characteristics of Frequent Pornography Users

The majority of the above mentioned concerns about pornography involve children who frequently view pornography online. Obviously, not all teens are frequent users of pornography. Many are only occasional users. The question then becomes, what makes a youth a frequent viewer of pornography? Researchers have also been curious about this and there are some recent research articles on the subject.

In a 2014 study of Swedish youth, the investigators looked at various factors that affected voluntary pornography consumption among teens. The authors found that the girls in the studied group of teens who consumed a lot of pornography frequently did not live with both parents. These girls lived with one parent or alternated between parents. These girls also self reported that the family financial situation was more difficult than the girls in the non-frequent user group. The youth in this study who were frequent watchers of pornography had poorer psychosocial health than the other teens. They also reported problematic relationships with their parents. In particular, the boys tended to have overprotective, controlling fathers. They also found that children who had conflicts with parents were more vulnerable to online grooming and sexual solicitation online. Several other studies have confirmed the link between poor family ties or relationships and frequent online pornography use. Other studies have found that youth who are frequent pornography users have poor social ties to church, school or family.

Other studies have looked at the particular family dynamic and how it affects attitudes about pornography and sexually explicit media. These studies have found several interesting things. Not surprisingly, families that treat sex as a taboo subject and don't talk about sex at all are making their children more susceptible to be influenced by online sexually explicit content. Additionally, people who are brought up in families that do not have much education around sexuality are also more vulnerable to the influences of online pornography.

The findings here are not surprising. What influences teens' use of sexually explicit media? Poor family relationships. Poor communication with parents. Lack of parental sex education and treating sexuality as a taboo subject. There is one really beautiful thing about these research findings. Most of the things that influence a child's susceptibility to online sexual content are changeable. Parents can educate themselves about sex and sexuality. Parents and children can work to improve their communication with each other and improve their relationships. Parents who are divorced or separated can, knowing that their child may be at higher risk, hopefully work together to co-parent in a healthy manner. The one downside here is that parents tend to have their own "stuff" around sex and sexuality. That too is changeable and we will talk about parent's "stuff" in a later chapter.

Pornography Induced Erectile Dysfunction

The concept of Pornography Induced Erectile Dysfunction was first talked about by an Italian medical doctor, Dr. Carlos Foresta. This doctor was seeing a number of cases of erectile dysfunction in young men. These men were much younger than the normal onset of erectile issues and they were all medically healthy. Dr. Foresta has continued to study this issue. One of the things that he found in his early work is that many of these young, physically healthy men who had issues with sexual functioning were frequent consumers of pornography.

The concept of pornography induced erectile dysfunction (PIED) is a controversial one. Despite the controversy, there is a growing body of research that suggests that the phenomenon is real. One of the best non-academic resources on PIED is a website called www.yourbrainonporn.com. This website is curated by Gary Wilson and he has written a book by the same name. www. Yourbrainonporn.com is a go to resource for myself and many others when we are teaching or lecturing about the effects of pornography consumption on the adolescent brain. Not only does this website keep up to date on the latest research on the topic but there are a series of very well put together videos on topics related to the subject, such as Adolescent Brain Meets High Speed Porn. I highly suggest that anyone interested in the topic check out the website and watch the videos. They are also great resources for adolescents to watch as well.

What is pornography induced erectile dysfunction? PIED is sometimes found in young men who started to look at online pornography at a young age. These young men also tend to watch a considerable amount of online pornography. These men, who started showing up in both doctors' offices and online forums showed similar symptoms. They had unexplained erectile dysfunction, meaning they were healthy young men with no physical reason to have any ED. These young men also experienced delayed ejaculation. Other signs of PIED include a declining interest in real partners. That is to say, when experiencing an interaction with a live, in person man or woman, the man with PIED is not as aroused or excited at the prospect of sex with a real person. They do not, however, have this lack of physical arousal when interacting with pornography.

A final common symptom that often occurs in these young men is an escalation in the type of pornography that they watch. For example, they may start out watching some traditional heterosexual themed pornography. The longer they watch online pornography, the more bored they may get with the type of pornography that they are viewing. To use psychological lingo, the person watching a lot of pornography becomes desensitized to what they are watching. In order to get the same "zing" (my word), arousal or feeling from the pornography, they need to ramp up the zing. This is what we call escalation. For example, a teen who starts to frequently look at traditional pornography will quickly get desensitized to the imagery. He will then look for something more exciting. Perhaps he will look at pornography depicting threesomes, group sex or lesbians (assuming a heterosexual boy). Once he becomes desensitized to this type of imagery, he might then escalate to pornography depicting fetishes, bondage, coercion or rape. For some, when there is just nothing left that is exciting or arousing, the ultimate taboo is child pornography. What can be seen in the escalation is that these young men eventually end up being turned on by things that they originally found very unappealing or not arousing. Their arousal template was changed due to desensitization and escalation.

Another concern with early exposure to online pornography that can effect in person relationships involves the development of arousal templates. Research published on this topic, mostly using rats and mice, lends credence to the idea that arousal templates can be created. As this book is not intended to be a scientific review of these topics, I will not touch on them here. What I can do is provide a case example.

Several years ago I worked with a lovely young man who was about 17 years old. He was very intelligent and kind. He came to treatment because he was having issues with online pornography (mostly YouTube) and video game addiction. The type of pornography that his young man was drawn to was not traditional pornography. He watched anime and manga pornography. Pornography in these arenas does not involve real people but drawings or animation. The men and women in these videos or images tend to have very cartoonish characteristics such as brightly colored hair as well as very amplified sexual organs. This young man's arousal template made it very difficult to engage with live girls his age. He was attracted to young women, with very large eyes, bright purple hair and unusually large breasts. Fundamentally, he was aroused to a cartoon version of a woman and not the real thing.

This arousal template has been discussed much more frequently in Japan, as there is a cultural movement of young people not being sexual and not wanting to engage in sexual relationships. A medical doctor in Japan, Dr. Kunio Kitamura, published a book entitled Young People Adverse to Sex. In his book he relates the thoughts of young Japanese men and women. He found that they often find it too much of a bother to have sex with another person. Additionally, he found that many of the young men preferred girls as anime characters. Many of the young men in the study preferred to have their sexual needs met by themselves via masturbation.

Though PIED might not seem as though it is a major concern to parents of young adolescent men, it is something that can cause future relationship issues as well as mental health issues such as anxiety and depression. It is obviously up to the individuals themselves if they want to have a relationship with another person and I make no judgment there. However, when individuals decide that they do want to date or have a relationship, their past or current frequent use of pornography may make having a satisfying sexual relationship with their partner very difficult.

The Legal Aspects of a Teen's Digital Sexual Consumption

In this chapter, we have reviewed the possible effects of sexting, cybersex and online pornography on adolescents. Though the body of research is small, it all points to the frequent consumption of digital sexual imagery having some profound impacts on youth, their developing attitudes, beliefs and arousal templates. Those teens who frequently use online sexual imagery have more permissive and risky attitudes about sex. They tend to objectify women and the act of sex itself more than non-frequent users of online pornography. Teens may end up with a very distorted view of actual sex and have body image issues or performance issues if they don't measure up to "porn sex." Teens might end up with a compulsive problem with pornography or masturbation. They might also end up in legal trouble, which we will talk about in the next chapter.

The one main factor that stands out in the research is that these problems tend to occur for those teens who use pornography or online sexual imagery FREQUENTLY. A child who sometimes watches Internet pornography or engages in sex chat is not necessarily going to end up with these issues. Viewing pornography is a normative adolescent behavior and has been since before the advent of easy Internet access. The explosion of technology means that this normative process is now an online process for most. The occasional user most likely won't have any problems. However, the frequent user might end up having adverse effects from watching digital pornography.

As a parent, it is your job to engage with your child, talk about the issues and help deter them from becoming a frequent user of digital sexual imagery.

Chapter 4

●●●●●●●●

Teens, Cybersex and The Law

The digital generation has to deal with one possible consequence of online pornography use and communication that pre-digital generations did not experience.

That is potential issues with the law. Prior to the Internet, in order to get pornography, someone had to buy the magazine or video. That meant, he or she had to go to the regular video store and go in the back room to get an adult film. Perhaps they had to go to an adult book store to get a magazine or movie. In some cases, a person would grab the magazine at the convenience store from the top rack that was half covered. In all instances, prior to the inception of child pornography laws, most people could only obtain legal pornography and it was mostly purchased face to face. If someone wanted illegal pornography, it was MUCH harder to obtain and often involved mail order from an obscure European vendor.

Digital natives face several potential legal pitfalls if they are sexting, looking at online pornography or taking consensual pictures of themselves with their sexual partners. We will discuss each of these issues separately as the different types of behaviors can fall under different laws.

My clinical practice focuses almost completely on working with sexual addictions. Many clients are addicted to pornography, specifically, online pornography. As I continued to work in the field, I began working more frequently with men who were being investigated for and ultimately convicted for possessing child pornography, or what we, in the field, call images of child sexual abuse. Seven or eight years ago, all of the men that I worked with in this capacity were at least in their 30s, and the majority of these men were in their late 40s, 50s or even older. The older offenders frequently started looking at pornography at a young age but first viewed print magazines and then movies. They moved to Internet pornography with the advent--not necessarily just of computers--but with the appearance of high speed Internet connections. At some point in their addiction, their behavior escalated and they began watching images of child sexual assault.

The longer I do this work, the younger my clients present in age. Now it is not uncommon for a new client coming into treatment for possession of child pornography to be 19, 20 or 21 years old. Where it used to be mostly older men, now it is frequently young men, very young men. These young men frequently started viewing pornography online at the age of 11 or 12 years old. At that time, they came across images of young girls or boys, girls or boys their own age. Though possessing or downloading these images was/is illegal, these boys (all of my legal clients to date have been male) were looking at sexual images that were age appropriate at that time. As the boys aged into older teens or young men, often, they continued to view these images of younger children in images of child sexual assault. Eventually, they come to the attention of law enforcement and have to face the consequences. At times, these young men are under 18 at the time they are investigated. Arrests and convictions for possession of child pornography can and frequently do have dire and lifelong consequences for the convicted person.

Why, in a book about digital sexuality for teens, am I talking about child pornography and sex offenders? Depending on the state in which you and your child live, if they engage in sexting or viewing of online pornography, they may be at risk for legal action involving laws designed to protect children. A child who gets in trouble for sexting naked images of themselves can be arrested for producing child pornography and distributing child pornography at the same time that they would be considered the victim of child pornography. This makes absolutely no sense to anyone informed about digital technology who understands digital natives. However, the law is often very slow to catch up to technology. Some states have no laws against sexting. Some states have eased up the punishments for teens sexting while others still have harsh sentences for the practice.

According to the Law Street website, some states have been adopting teen sexting laws. The adoption of these laws began in 2009. At the time of the writing of this book, the states that currently have laws on the books regarding sexting include: Arizona, Arkansas, Connecticut, Florida, Georgia, Hawaii, Illinois, Louisiana, Nebraska, Nevada, New Jersey, New York, North Dakota, Texas, Utah, Vermont, and West Virginia. However, not all of these states have laws that apply to both the sending and receiving of sexual images by minors.

My practice is in the Commonwealth of Pennsylvania, so I will start with the laws in this state first. As we discuss the laws regarding sexting in each state, please remember that I am not a lawyer and my understanding of these laws comes from my reading of them and not from any legal knowledge in the form of legal practice.

Pennsylvania

Teen sexting laws were enacted in Pennsylvania in October of 2012. The official verbiage of the law is the "Transmission of sexually explicit images by a minor." The type of sexting is broken down into several categories. It is a summary offense for a minor to distribute, transmit or publish a sexually explicit image of him or herself. It is also a summary offense to knowingly possess a sexually explicit image of a minor who is 12 or older. If a minor distributes a sexual image of another minor who is 12 years or older, they will be charged with a third degree misdemeanor.

The prior two offenses could be said to apply to consensual sexting, or sexting between two people in a relationship. The Pennsylvania law distinguishes between this and sexting with harmful intent. It is a second degree misdemeanor for a minor to take a sexual image or distribute a sexual image of another minor 12 or older without their consent and/or for the purposes of coercion, intimidation, harassment, or torment or to cause emotional distress.

This part of the law addresses third party sexting that can be part of cyber-bullying. The Pennsylvania law does have a few provisos that can change the outcome. If the sext image contains "conduct that involves images that depict sexual intercourse, deviate sexual intercourse, or penetration however slight of the genitals or anus of a minor, masturbation, sadism, masochism, or bestiality," the sexting law may not apply. Additionally, any image that was taken for commercial purposes will not be prosecuted under this law. Basically, if the sext contains an image that is of a nude minor, then the lesser offenses apply. If the image is of an actual sex act, the lesser offenses do not apply and the minor can be charged under child pornography statutes. If a minor is convicted of the summary offense or the misdemeanors, they can be sentenced to attend an educational program as part of a diversionary program. If the teen completes this course and diversion, their record is expunged.

New Jersey

Our neighboring state of New Jersey has taken a different approach to deal with teen sexting. New Jersey created a diversionary program for juveniles who are charged with sexting or posting sexual images. Each case is to be reviewed and judged on a number of criteria to determine if the teen is eligible for the diversionary program. The court looks at the following criteria: How serious was the offense? How old is the juvenile and how mature is he or she? Does the teen pose a risk to others? What are the family influences? For example, is there a family history of abuse, drug or alcohol abuse or other issues in the family? Has the teen made use of services such as counseling? What are the recommendations of the prosecutor, the arresting officer and the victim? In my opinion, a program such as this is a better option than a cookie cutter approach. It makes sense to treat those teens who are consensually sexting differently than those who are using images for bullying or who are disseminating pictures without the knowledge of the victim.

Arizona

In Arizona, the laws depend on the context of the sexting, meaning the number of people a child sends a sext to can determine the penalty. Arizona also does take into account the fact that sometimes children do not always request these images and does not penalize children who didn't want a picture, deleted it or reported the sext to the authorities. The law defines these acts as the unlawful use of a communication device. In Arizona it is illegal for a juvenile to intentionally or knowingly use an electronic communication device, phone, computer, etc, to send or possess sexual images of children. It also unlawful for the juvenile to possess an image sent to him or her. If a child breaks these laws, it is considered a petty offense if the transmission is to one person alone. If the juvenile sends the image to more than one person, this is considered a class 3 misdemeanor. It appears as though this is the law's way of differentiating consensual sexting from non-consensual disseminating. If a teen sexts her boyfriend and gets caught, it is a petty offense. If they break up and the boyfriend sends the text to all his friends, this is then considered a misdemeanor. Juveniles are not in violation of any law if they did not solicit the image or if they destroyed the image and reported it to an authority figure. If a teen is caught for a second time, the petty offense moves to a misdemeanor.

Arkansas

In August of 2013, Arkansas enacted a law to address teen sexting. The law states that a juvenile commits the offense of possessing sexually explicit material when they "purposely create, transmit, distribute, presents, transmits, posts, exchanges, disseminates, or possesses through a computer, wireless communication device, or digital media, any sexually explicit material. " The language of the Arkansas law is interesting as it explicitly states "posting" so that posts to social medial are included in this offense. There are a number of means in which a juvenile could not be charged with this offense. If the child has not solicited the image, did not distribute it and destroys the image, the child will not be charged. The minor also will not be charged with this crime if the child created the image and did not distribute it. This offense is a class A misdemeanor in Arkansas. An adolescent found guilty can be offered eight hours of community service for a first offense.

Connecticut

Connecticut enacted their legislation regarding sexting in 2010. The law applies to teens who are 13 years of age or older but under the age of 18. The language of the Connecticut law does not include sexting itself but uses the term child pornography. In this state, no child 13-17 years old may knowingly possess any visual depiction of child pornography that the subject of the image knowingly and voluntarily transmitted. Additionally, no child 13-17 can knowingly or voluntarily transmit an image depicting child pornography. If a minor between the ages of 13 and 17 violates this law in Connecticut, the child will be guilty of a class A misdemeanor.

Florida

Florida enacted laws related to sexting in 2011. The language of their law specifically states sexting a juvenile in Florida breaks the law if the child knowingly transmits an image of nudity or possesses a sexual image of another minor. In Florida, as in other states, the juvenile is not in violation of the law if the child did not ask for the image or transmit the image and reported the incident to some authority. Florida's sexting law combines any number of images sent in a 24-hour period into one offense, as opposed to counting each image as a possible offense. This part of the law makes sense in that if a teenage couple are interacting back and forth via text and sending images, the chances are that multiple images may be sent in a day's time. This law breaks things down into what I will call incidents of sexting not individual images. Florida juveniles who are convicted of this offense for the first time are given a non-criminal violation and can be made to perform community service and/or attend an educational class on the subject. They also have to pay a $60.00 fine. If a juvenile re-offends, he or she is charged with a misdemeanor for the second offense and a felony for the third offense.

Georgia

In 2013, Georgia enacted legislation to address sexting. House Bill 156 specifically states that the bill is to modernize the laws relating to sexual conduct and technology. It also specifically states that its goal is to reduce the punishment of particular crimes that are committed by children. This law is a bit confusing for the lay person to read and decipher. For sexting incidents where the individual is at least 14 years of age and the image was created with the permission or consent of the minor, possession of the image is a misdemeanor. If the image is distributed, the penalty could be harsher. Felony charges could be brought against the juvenile if they used the images to embarrass, threatened or harass the person depicted in the image. Ultimately, it appears to be up to the court's discretion as to how the juvenile is ultimately charged.

Hawaii

Hawaii has enacted legislation specifically addressing sexual images produced by minors. This state calls the offense "promoting minor-produced sexual images." It is illegal for a minor to knowingly use a computer, cell phone or other electronic device to send or distribute a nude image of his or herself or another person. It is also illegal to command, request or encourage another minor to take and send a nude picture to the requester. The law does allow for what it calls an affirmative defense if the person in possession of the nude picture of the minor took steps to destroy the image. This offense is a petty misdemeanor.

Illinois

The law regulating sexting by minors in Illinois does not specifically address the possession of an image of a minor in regard to sexting, but does make the dissemination of an "indecent visual depiction" via electronic means illegal. If convicted of violating this law a minor may be sentenced to counseling and/or community service.

Louisiana

The southern state of Louisiana has created legislation to address sexting as well. In this state, anyone who is younger than 17 years of age cannot use any electronic device to transmit indecent images they take of themselves. It is also illegal for a minor to transmit or send indecent images of someone else. The state has a wide array of penalties they can impose for first time juvenile offenders. Among other things, the court can impose a sentence of house arrest and community service. Additionally, the teen may have to pay a fine. If the same juvenile reoffends, the penalties increase and the youth could face up to six months in jail.

Nebraska

In Nebraska, it is a felony for anyone to possess or distribute sexual images of a child. Their sexting laws fall under this statute. A minor may not be charged with this crime if several conditions are met. First, the image in the juvenile's possession must be of a minor who is at least 15 years of age. Second, the image must have been voluntarily made and provided to the possessor. The image cannot contain more than one other minor. Also, the juvenile must NOT have distributed the image to anyone else nor pressured the sender of the image to send sexual content. If the juvenile in possession of a sext does not meet these criteria, they will be prosecuted.

Nevada

Nevada's law pertaining to sexting prohibits, under certain circumstances, the possession, transmission or distribution of certain sexual images. If a minor sends a picture of him or herself to another person, they may be determined to be delinquent. Again, as in most states, these laws apply to a nude photo and not images of a sex act. If a minor sends an image of a sex act, oral sex for example, they can be prosecuted according to the law, deemed a sex offender and be required to register as such. The difference between penalties is enormous. A sexy picture will cause the teen a bit of trouble but an image of actual sex acts can ruin their lives.

New York

The law in New York is a bit different from other state's laws. In New York, the juvenile sexting law applies to individuals under the age of 20 years old. In New York, both the sender and the receiver of a nude image stand to deal with some consequences. However, if they are both under twenty years old and within five years of age from one another, they can be sentenced to an 8 hour educational program as opposed to facing harsher legal consequences.

North Dakota

North Dakota's law does not explicitly apply to minors but does appear to apply to sexting in general. The crime in this state is a misdemeanor. It is unlawful to possess a sexually expressive image without consent of the sender (addressing perhaps sexts that get distributed without consent to others). It is also unlawful to distribute an image both without consent and with any intent to cause emotional harm or humiliation. What I truly like about the language of this law is its statement about expectation of privacy. The law states that "without written consent from each individual who has a reasonable expectation of privacy in the image...." It is my belief that most juveniles who send a sexual image of themselves to a partner or potential partner have an expectation of privacy, and this law addresses that specifically.

Rhode Island

The law in Rhode Island addresses the transmission of an image but not the possession of an image. It is unlawful for a minor to knowingly and voluntarily send an indecent image of him or herself to another person. The law only applies if the image was sent without threat or coercion. This is an important caveat to the law as some minors feel pressured or forced to send images. Additionally, it is known that some of the youth produced sexual imagery found online was coerced by someone on the other side of a webcam or chat. In these instances, there is no violation of the law. If a minor does break this law, they are given a status offense and it is handled in family court. The law explicitly states that the minor is not subject to sex offender registration.

South Dakota

South Dakota, similar to other states, considers possession or distribution of sexual images of a minor by a minor to be illegal. In this state it is a misdemeanor. A minor may not be charged if they did not ask for the sexual image, did not send the sexual image and/or deleted the image.

Texas

The Texas legal code specifically addresses sexting by a minor. In Texas, it is illegal to possess sexual imagery of a child. A minor in Texas can break this law if he or she knowingly "promotes" to another minor any visual image that depicts a minor (including the person in the picture) engaging in sexual conduct. This law applies to a minor who took the image or knows the person who did. It is also illegal to possess these images. The penalties for breaking this law are variable. The punishment for a minor is a Class C misdemeanor. However, that can be increased to a higher level misdemeanor if the minor has been previously convicted for the same crime. The minor may not be prosecuted if the image portrayed only the minor him or herself or one other minor, if the other minor is within two years of age of the juvenile who is being prosecuted. Additionally, they may not be prosecuted if they are married. Additionally, a minor may not be prosecuted if she or he did not solicit the image and destroyed the image.

Utah

Utah's laws were laid out in 2009 in the Material Harmful to Minors Amendments. The bill was created to modify the law in Utah regarding distribution of pornography and material harmful to minors. In Utah the distribution of pornographic material is illegal with exemptions for Internet service providers. In this state the law is violated if: a person brings pornography into the state with the intent to distribute; prepares, publishes or prints pornography with the intent to distribute; distributes, offers to distribute or exhibits pornographic material; writes, creates or solicits the publication or advertising of pornographic material; distributes, exhibits or promotes any material the person says is pornographic; or presents or directs a pornographic performance. If someone over 18 commits one of these offenses, they will receive a third degree felony. If the person who commits this crime is 16 or 17 years old they receive a Class A misdemeanor and if they are under 16 years of age they receive a Class B misdemeanor. However, a second offense by a juvenile is a felony. Utah's laws regarding pornography are rather strict when compared to the laws for other states. What I find interesting is that in reading this bill, the Internet service providers are rather exempt from this law. In today's age, parts of this law feel a bit outdated. Most pornography is entering homes via some mobile device and shared via an Internet provider. If a state really wants to keep out all pornography, this is a pretty big exemption.

Vermont

Vermont law states that it is illegal for a minor to voluntarily send an indecent image of him or herself to another. It is also illegal to possess said image. Again, as with many states, if a minor destroyed the image, they likely will not be prosecuted. A first time offender will be dealt with in family court. They may have to attend a juvenile diversion program. The law also explicitly states that a first time offender shall NOT be processed under the sexual exploitation of children and will NOT be required to register as a sex offender. A minor who is a repeat offender may be prosecuted under laws relating to the sexual exploitation of a minor but again, the law states that they will NOT be subject to sex offender registration. I applaud Vermont for explicitly stating in its law that a minor is not required to register as a sex offender. The research regarding juvenile sex offender registration does not support its use as being effective.

West Virginia

The final state that currently has legislation specific to minor sexting is West Virginia. West Virginia law states that juveniles are not to manufacture, possess or distribute nude or partially nude images of minors. If they are found to violate this law, it is to be considered an act of delinquency. The law that was passed in 2013 (H.B. 2357) created a diversion program for juveniles. The court itself has the ability to decide if the juvenile will be placed on the sex offender registry. This law also lays out the topics to be covered in the diversion program. The topics that must be included in the diversion training program for minors include: the non-legal consequences of sexting; long term consequences of the Internet (it never goes away); information on cyberbullying; and the legal consequences. A final piece of this law is that it also makes the creation of videos by minors, of minors, illegal.

Additional States Considering Laws

In the time it has taken to write this book, several states have been working on legislation to deal with the issue of teen sexting. The most recent states to do this are Colorado and Idaho. After a well-publicized sexting scandal hit the Canon City schools in Colorado, some lawmakers sought to amend the laws that they perceived as too harsh. The law as it stands in Colorado considers the possession of sexual images of a minor a felony and require sex offender registration. This law stands regardless of the age of the person possessing the images.

Bipartisan lawmakers in Colorado proposed House Bill 1058. This bill would make it a Class 2 misdemeanor for a juvenile to distribute, display, publish or possess any sexually explicit image of a minor. It also provided an affirmative defense for any minor who was sent images he or she did not request or if they took steps to get rid of the images (Denver Post, April 4, 2016). This bill did not pass in the Colorado state senate on April 5, 2016. Those lawmakers who rejected the bill had concerns about protecting victims of non-consensual sexting. It is thought that the Colorado law makers will continue to work on this issue and new legislation may be proposed soon.

In March 2016, lawmakers in Idaho passed an amended sexting bill that created a distinction between minors engaging in sexting and adults possessing child pornography images. This bill classifies sexting by a minor as a misdemeanor. At present, any sexting done by a juvenile is treated the same as an adult. A juvenile would face prison time and become a registered sex offender. The Idaho bill allows law enforcement to charge a minor with a felony for sexting if they repeatedly send sexual content to a large number of people. This bill is awaiting the approval of Idaho's Governor.

In March 2016, Kentucky lawmakers considered and passed Senate bill 37. This bill lessens the penalty for sexting among juveniles from a felony to a misdemeanor. Repeat juvenile offenders would be subjected to a more severe class of misdemeanor but still would not have a felony conviction that would place them on a sex offender registry.

Other states are also looking at sexting as a form of cyberbullying. In March 2016, California proposed Assembly Bill 2536 which would allow schools the ability to expel a student who is engaging in non-consensual sexting. This bill specifically addresses sexting for the purpose of humiliating or harassing a student. This bill allows schools to enact non-legal discipline for sexting that is non-consensual. Those who oppose the proposed law would prefer that students who are caught engaging in this type of sexting be able to stay in school but also undergo counseling.

The following states have no specific legislation relating to teen sexting at the time of this writing: Alabama, Alaska, California, Delaware, Indiana, Iowa, Kansas, Kentucky, Maine, Maryland, Massachusetts, Michigan, Minnesota, Mississippi, Missouri, Montana, New Hampshire, New Mexico, North Carolina, Ohio, Oklahoma, Oregon, South Carolina, Tennessee, Virginia, Washington, Wisconsin, Wyoming, and the District of Columbia.

So what then happens to teens in these states if they are found to be sexting or in possession of sexual images of another minor?

To answer this question, I turn to an event that occurred on April 2, 2015. A news story broke about two Joliet, Illinois teens found to have sexted images of sexual conduct. The police chief decided that the best course of action was to charge these two minors (between the age of 14 and 16, who were in a relationship together) with child pornography charges. This seems counter to the fact that the state of Illinois does, in fact, have a teen sexting law.

Here is an extremely important fact. The majority of the laws that are in place regarding teen sexting in all states apply only to nude or sexually suggestive images. These laws do NOT apply to images or videos that are sent that depict actual sex acts. The legal consequences for sending a nude solo image are significantly less than for sending a picture of even consensually photographed or videoed sexual intercourse, oral sex or even, sometimes, masturbation. The police chief in this Illinois case wanted to make sure that he sent a clear message that society will not accept this type of behavior and he wanted the punishment to act as a deterrent to other teenagers and encourage them to not create photographic evidence of their sexual encounters.

This brings us to the topic of minors being arrested and convicted for the production, distribution and possession of child pornography. This happens in several different manners. One way in which these teens get in trouble for possessing this imagery is similar to what is stated above. The first route is through consensual imagery that is created between two minors in a relationship. If they get caught with the images, perhaps one parent finds them on their child's phone and reports it, they can be arrested under laws regarding sexual imagery of children. Another route also involves sexting but not necessarily the consensual kind. We have spoken earlier about how an image that was sent consensually might end up making the rounds at a high school or through a group of friends. This type of sexting is not consensual and is often done without the knowledge of the original sender. Again, depending on whether the image is a sex act versus sexually suggestive as well as whether or not the state has sexting or revenge porn laws, this behavior can end up a violation of laws relating to the possession of images of child sexual assault.

There is another avenue through which a minor might be in legal trouble with child pornography. This is what I would call the more traditional route, and it is similar to how an adult might end up in violation of child pornography laws. As I have stated earlier in this book, part of my clinical work involves working with men who have violated child pornography possession laws. These men (I have not yet had any female clients for this issue) have viewed images of child sexual abuse online. A traditional trajectory for my clients (though I am sure not of all who possess these images) is that they start out watching more traditional pornography online and end up escalating to more taboo subjects and many end up looking at illegal images of children.

Young Offenders

What I want to focus on here are the younger people. The younger generation of offenders I work with started out looking at pornography online around 12 years old. Many of these young men were looking at images of boys or girls their age. This ends up being a bit of a conundrum. If a 12 year old is looking at another 12 or 13 year old in a sexual fashion, this is actually age appropriate. They are sexualizing their peers online as they would do in person, at a school function or fantasizing while in class. The MAJOR problem with this is that the images they are looking at, though age appropriate, are highly illegal. In my practice, I have yet to have any minors in treatment who were arrested for possession of child pornography from this route. I have had young adults (20-year-olds) who were arrested as adults but started looking at the illegal imagery when they were the same age as the children in the images.

The point of this book is not to be political or preachy about the laws regarding sexting and child pornography possessions. The laws were created for possession, production and distribution sexual images of children for one purpose. They were created to protect children. This, obviously, is a critical objective. In the field we often refer to the imagery as child sexual abuse instead of child pornography. Many of the images of children are clearly of child sexual assault. Everyone involved needs to be punished so that children can be safe. However, sexual images created by two consenting 16-year-old minors, for example, are not images of child sexual assault. They are sexual images that two consensual teenagers created that violated a very serious law. These types of images do not fit the spirit of the law--protecting abused children.

If a minor is arrested and convicted for child pornography possession, it can have serious consequences that last a lifetime. In May of 2013, Human Rights Watch published a document entitled Raised on the Registry: The irreparable harm of placing children on sex offender registries. I received a copy of this report at the 2013 annual conference of the Association for the Treatment of Sexual Abusers. I have always tried to base my opinions about these types of topics on scientific data, and even prior to reading this report, I was against lifetime registry for juveniles.

Many states have laws that place juveniles convicted of sexual offenses on a sex offender registry that is exactly the same as the registry for adults. Some states have policies that require a juvenile arrested for a sexual offense to be on the registry for the rest of his or her life. For example, if a 12-year-old boy is convicted in juvenile court of something that will place him on the juvenile sex offender registry, he may, depending on where he lives, have to register as a sex offender for the rest of his life. He could, perhaps, have to register as a sex offender for the next 70 to 80 years. The experience of my adult sex offenders tells me that being on the registry makes it nearly impossible to get a job and even more impossible to get a job making enough money to truly support themselves and surely not enough to support a family.

The impact on a juvenile who is on the sex offender registry is severe. The impact also crosses many parts of life. First, there is the potential for a great deal of psychological harm to these children. They are often shunned, stigmatized, socially isolated and frequently very depressed. Many juveniles who are on the registry contemplate, attempt or commit suicide. There is also a very significant psychological impact to the parents of the child on the sex offender registry. The children and their families have been known to receive very serious harassment and even threats of physical harm.

There are also many logistical impacts of a juvenile being on the sex offender registry. Some children may not be able to go to school, as there might be restrictions regarding a sex offender being at or near a school. This means that the parents will either have to find another school such as a cyberschool or will have to home school their children. This becomes more difficult if a child is restricted from using the Internet.

Youth sex offenders, just like adult sex offenders, often have an extremely hard time finding employment. Most employers will not hire someone on the sex offender registry. Actual housing for the entire family may also become a problem. Again, depending on the state, there may be residency restrictions for a registered sex offender. If the family's home is too close to a school, park, day care, etc., the child may not be able to live there. That means that he or she either cannot live with the parents, or the entire family has to move. Additionally, if there are other children in the home, the offender may not be able to live in the house either, as a very common restriction is no unsupervised contact with a minor, even if that other minor is a family member.

I am not a big fan of scare tactics as I don't really think fear works as a long term deterrent of behavior. That being said, I realize that the prior information may sound like something designed to engender fear. But this chapter is a necessity based in reality. What we know from science is that even though teens know that they can get in legal trouble for sexting, that knowledge does not really deter them from engaging in the behavior. I don't think that teens really understand the impact of the consequences until they are smack dab in the middle of them. I honestly don't think that parents understand the consequences either. There are frequently news stories about teen sexting and scandal. These stories often do discuss the potential consequences that the teens are facing but I have never seen one of these stories discuss what it actually means for his or her family when a teen is charged with this crime, convicted and then have to deal with the long term consequences. These consequences have the potential to last a lifetime.

Though I know that fear of consequences is not going to deter all or maybe even most of the behavior by teens, it is still valuable knowledge for parents to have. When you talk to your child about sexting and online pornography, this needs to be part of the discussion. The desire to go to Harvard law school or to be a police officer or to enter the military can be completely dashed with one press of the send button.

Chapter 5

●●●●●●●●●

What's My "Stuff?"
How Do Your Beliefs Influence
How You Talk to your Child
About Cybersex?

There are many things that affect how a parent does or does not talk to their children about sex and sexuality. The list is long. Some parents themselves lack sufficient knowledge of sexual development to be informative to their children. Many parents find the thought of having in depth discussions of sex and relationships awkward and uncomfortable. They don't know what to say. They assume that their children are getting sufficient sex education in school. They are embarrassed about talking to their child about sex. They don't want to deal with their child's reaction to "the talk." Parents can also avoid discussions of sex and sexuality due to their own issues with sex, including histories of sexual abuse and shame. Lastly, what parents do and do not talk about to their children may be based on their religious beliefs. My goal in this chapter is to discuss the various reasons why parents don't talk to their children and offer some thoughts on how to address these issues.

A few days ago I was in the office on a Saturday doing paperwork and ran into a colleague that I don't often see. He asked me for my thoughts and advice on a client he is seeing. My colleague is seeing a young man, about 16 years old, who is struggling with a severe online pornography addiction. The young man had previously gotten in trouble (not legal) for having sexual images of peers on his phone. The young man was sexting. This young man is very distraught about his struggle with ceasing pornography use. He and his family come from a rather conservative religious background and his actions cause a direct conflict in his mind with his religious belief, causing what we call in the field, cognitive dissonance.

I am not relating this story to talk about the teen, however, but his parents. My colleague's greatest struggle in treating this young man is the parents. The young man's parents have tried to filter and monitor his technology, and he finds a way around it. This is normal addictive behavior. When the parents find out he has relapsed, they use a very punitive, critical method to talk to him. His behavior goes against their religious beliefs. They feel that any type of pornography is wrong. They are currently unable to have a conversation with their son about his pornography use that is not shaming and demeaning. They are actually making the problem worse and exacerbating his shame spiral. The inability of the parents in this case to talk about sex and pornography in a non-judgmental or negative way is directly, negatively impacting their son.

I am not saying that they need to abandon their religious beliefs or their moral philosophies. What I am saying is that the parents' beliefs are getting in the way of productive parenting in the digital sexual age.

A recent study published in the open access journal, *BMJ Open*, looked at the sources of information about sex among young Britons and provided some interesting findings. One of the findings of the study is a direct hit on what I am talking about in this book. In the United Kingdom, schools must teach a sex and relationship education class that covers the biological pieces of sex, such as puberty and reproduction, as well as information about sexually transmitted diseases and HIV/AIDS. Government run schools there are now also required to teach more aspects of sex and relationships such as those that are personal or social. However, for this part of sex and relationship education, there is no set curriculum. The study states there is some advice about what should be taught in these courses. The topics include: safe use of technology, the impact of pornography use, sexual consent and abuse and violence in relationships. These guidelines sound very forward thinking and necessary given the world we live in today.

There is one finding of this study that really stands out to me. The young people in this survey wanted more information about sex and relationships. Not only did they want more information about sex and relationships, but they wanted it from their parents. When asked what their source of information about sex was, few children stated it was their parents, though these same children stated that a parent was their preferred choice to talk to about sex and relationships. Young men, in particular, wanted more information to have come from their parents.

The results of this recent study show how parents are, in a way, failing their children when it comes to talking about sex and relationships. Though there is a stigma about "the talk" with mom or dad about sex and relationships, it turns out that, despite protests, this is what kids really want. Parents who let their own "stuff" get in the way of talking to their children about sex end up relying on a school curriculum to do so. Do parents even know what the school is teaching in their sexual education curriculum? Are they only talking about biology or are they also talking about relationships, pornography, sexting and other things that are relevant to today's world?

Why Parents Don't Talk to Their Kids about Sex

So let's look at some reasons why parents don't talk to their children about sex. Embarrassment may be the prime reason. Let's face it, talking about sex to your child is awkward. Even the best conversation starts out awkward. In September 2014, a British company, Lil-Lets, conducted a poll of parents asking them about how they feel about talking about sex to their children. The results are not surprising. The poll found that millions of parents struggled with these conversations. Some parents had hopes that the schools would take care of it and some parents avoided the conversations all together. In this study, over 60% of the British parents admitted that it was difficult to talk to their children about sensitive subjects. The study showed that 54% of the parents worried about how having a talk about sex would make their child feel. More than half of the parents surveyed dreaded the time when they would have to talk about sex to their child and one in five parents have had anxiety about the talk since their child was as young as even four years old. The study showed that 41% of parents had an argument about which parent was going to talk to their child about sex.

The worst part of the results, for me, is the fact that four in ten--or forty percent of parents--COMPLETELY avoided talking to their child about sex and relationships. A final result from this survey which we all need to remember is that over half the parents surveyed reported that they felt closer to their child after they sat down with them to have "the talk."

These 2014/2015 publications run counter to the results of a survey done by the Center for Latino Adolescent and Family Health in 2011. This survey of 1,111 moms and dads of children aged 10-18 stated that 82% of parents are talking to their children about sexual topics and sexuality. Less were comfortable talking about things like birth control and how to say no to sex. The survey does reiterate that when parents can effectively talk to their children about sexual topics, the children make safer decisions about sex. Studies show that these teens delay engaging in sex, are more likely to have safe sex and are more comfortable saying no to sex.

So, how do we account for mixed results? The difference is that the later studies in 2014 and 2015 asked about comfort in having the sex talk with kids as well as whether or not they were engaging in the talk. There could, perhaps be cultural differences between the UK and the United States. There could also be differences in the survey design and type of participants they found. This is one of the problems with science. No data is 100% perfect, and there can always be competing theories. Personally, the anecdotal data I have gathered from my work tells me that most parents are not comfortable talking about sex even if they do. Many of my client's parents either didn't have the talk or gave a cursory discussion that wasn't too meaningful.

The question remains, why are so many parents embarrassed or uncomfortable talking about sex? Sex is a natural part of human behavior and for all parents of non-adoptive children, they had sex in order to create their child. When sex and relationship educators talk to young people about sex, they often advise that they are not ready to have sex with a partner if they cannot talk about it. Well, with parents, we are a little past the "have sex" part but are still stuck on the talk about it.

Why is it hard to talk about sex with just about anyone and especially your kids? It's likely your "stuff." Stuff is my rather non-clinical word for the baggage that we all carry from our childhood, family of origin and experiences in life up to the point we are at today. Everyone has stuff. Stuff can come from family, church, school, friends, relationships, illness, abuse and a multitude of other things.

Let's start with family in general before we move into specific aspects of our experience. Here are some basic questions to ask yourself to identify what your "stuff" is about sex and sexuality.

First, how did your parents handle discussions about sex and sexuality with you when you were young? Did mom or dad or both sit down with you and talk about sex? Did anyone talk about sex? If so, what did they say to you and how? To help you start to dig into this process, let me share with you the family of origin experience of one of my clients. I asked him how he learned about sex and what his parents told him about sex. Here is the essence of his answer:

> *"My parents told me nothing of substance about sex. My father said absolutely nothing. One of my older brothers gave me a speech about using condoms and unwanted pregnancy. The scare tactic worked. Most of what I learned about sex was from my male friends or older boys in the neighborhood. We would discuss girls and sex among ourselves and the older boys would try to fill in the knowledge gaps for the younger boys. It was a completely male dominated discussion. When I was in elementary school, I found pornography magazines. These taught me about sexual positions and what a "man was supposed to do." I thought that I had to "get good at this and be like the men in the pictures."*

This story is from a Digital Immigrant male who then became addicted to Internet pornography. The story he relates is not uncommon. His parents didn't tell him anything about sex that he needed to know. He, at least, had a well-meaning older brother who at least taught him about birth control. He obtained his knowledge about sex from his peers and from pornography. The next question is: What messages did he receive about sex? In his youth, he received the following messages about sex.

1. **You don't talk about it. Since his parents didn't talk about sex with him, the implied message is that talking about sex is a taboo subject to be avoided. Children often infer more meaning from the implied message than the actual verbal message. In this family, sex is something that is secret.**

2. **The next message he received from his peers was that sex was something of a conquest. He told me that when he and his peers started to be sexual they would talk about it and would gain "bragging rights." This sends the message that sex is about sport and conquest and not necessarily about connection, intimacy and relationships.**

3. **He learned from pornography that sex is about performance. His own thoughts were that he "had to get good at this." Again, this reinforces the idea that sex is about performance and conquest as opposed to connection and intimacy.**

If, in your family, your parents were able to talk to you openly and freely, even if there was some awkwardness, you may have learned the message that sex is something that is ok to talk about. If you parents gave a bare bones discussion of the mechanics of the birds and the bees, you may have missed out on necessary discussions of sex and intimacy, relationships and the multitude of other issues that come up around sex in addition to the actual act. If your parents said nothing at all to you, you may have learned that sex is something that is NOT talked about. Sex is something that is supposed to be SECRET.

It may be helpful to take some time to sit down and really think about the messages you received from your family about sex. Answering these questions may help you understand what "stuff" your family gave you about discussing sex.

1. **Did your mom talk to you about sex? If so, what did she say?**

2. **Did your dad talk to you about sex? If so, what did he say?**

3. **Did any other primary caregiver talk to you about sex? What did they say?**

4. **Where did you learn about sex? School? Peers? Pornography? Movies?**

5. **What did school teach you about sex and relationships?**

6. **Did anyone talk to you about things other than the mechanics of sex? Birth control? Intimacy? Relationships? STDs? Knowing when you are ready to have sex?**

7. **What did you learn from your peers about sex?**

After spending time reflecting on the answers to these questions, ask yourself one final question. What messages did I get about sex and relationships from my family and peers? These messages are often both overt and implied. How then, do these messages influence how I either do or do not talk to my children about sexuality and relationships.

Sex and Religious Beliefs

Another part of a parent's "stuff" about sex and sexuality may come from the religious environment that they were raised in. Traditionally, children are not allowed to choose their religious affiliation nor their desire to participate in it until they are older. I am not saying this as a judgment of any religion or parental practice. Discussing religion can be a touchy topic. I don't make a stand on any particular religion as I have found with my clients, that if their beliefs help them in recovery and living an authentic life, it doesn't matter to me whether they are Christian, Muslim, Jewish, Buddhist, etc. I will talk here, generally, about how religious beliefs affect thoughts and feelings about sexuality.

In discussing the effects of early religious experience on beliefs about sexuality, I will draw on the experiences of my clients. Many of them have told me that their church or religion taught them as young people that sex was solely for the purpose of procreation. Most of my clients were also taught that sex outside of, or before marriage, was sinful. They were not to engage in sex until they were married. Many of my clients also received the message that masturbation was sinful as well. The messages that my clients received from their respective religious faiths often created internal turmoil for them. If I am a young, adolescent boy starting to have some sexual feelings toward others, does this make me bad? If I do end up masturbating, does this mean that I am now a sinner and God won't love me?

The conflict between biology and religious belief can create an enormous amount of conflict in a young person. As a child enters puberty and moves into adolescence, they start to have feelings of a sexual nature. They will start to notice others. They will start to have sexual thoughts. They might engage in masturbation. They might look at pornography. They may interact sexually with another young person their age. The child's biology is naturally going to be interested in sexual things. This creates a huge conflict for many children as they were taught by their faith that they are not supposed to have these feelings and if they have these feelings, they are not supposed to act on them until they are married. Additionally, if the child does act on these sexual feelings, they are going against their faith, creating anxiety or feelings of failure for some. One thing that this conflict often does is teach the adolescent that their sexual thoughts, feelings and actions must be kept secret and hidden. In order to not get in trouble or not be found out, sexuality moves into the shadows and becomes something that they don't talk about.

Another potential downfall of this internal conflict between biology and behavior is that, for some children, it creates an internalized sense of shame. If my faith is telling me that I should not be having these sexual feelings or that the sexual feelings are sinful and I am having these feelings, there must be something wrong with me. It is in this conflict that a child can start to feel shame for their sexual thoughts and feelings. Any number of things can add to this shame. I have had clients tell me that when they were young and were "caught" masturbating by a parent, they were told things like "God is watching you" or "God knows what you are doing." Statements such as this created such feelings of shame in my clients that they learned to hide all of their sexual thoughts, feelings and behaviors and came to see them as a shameful part of themselves.

Why is shame such a bad thing in this situation? We frequently say in addiction treatment that addiction lives in secrets and shame. That is why we encourage group therapy, disclosure and telling of the client's story, to reduce their shame. When sex is shamed and taught to be kept secret, we are creating the perfect environment for an addiction to form. It is one thing for mom or dad to be upset with what I am doing, and quite another entirely to go against God. The core beliefs of my addict clients tend to revolve around the idea that they are horrible, shameful people that no one would ever love if they were truly known. The idea that God thinks I am a bad person for perhaps masturbating makes me really bad. If God won't or can't love me, who will?

If, as an adult, this, or something similar, was your experience, how does that influence how you talk to your child(ren) about sex and sexuality? If you hold shame about sexuality, it is highly unlikely that you will be able to effectively talk to your child about these issues. If you were taught about sex via shaming messages, it is likely that you will then teach your children about sex in the same manner. Shame and messages of shame do not work when it comes to teaching about or discussing sex and sexuality. Another issue that can arise is that your religious beliefs about sex and sexuality might influence a level of denial. If you are teaching your child abstinence only per your faith, that does not actually mean that your child is listening. I have worked with several clients who taught this form of sex education and did not discuss digital sexuality, pornography, or anything else relevant to today's teens. These parents thought that their faith-based teaching combined with filtering the computer were enough. It turns out that this is normally not the case. The children of these families were looking at pornography in retail stores on the computers left out or looking at pornography at the houses of friends. And some of these children actually were having sex at church youth functions (at church) without education about sex itself or protection from pregnancy and disease.

If you received shameful messages about sex from your faith, it can influence your denial about the behaviors of your children.

Your Own Sexual History

When we are looking at our histories and the "stuff" that formed our beliefs about sex and sexuality, it is best to do so without judgment. Introspection about our history and how it formed our beliefs and influenced our behavior is not about blame but about self discovery. If you can come to understand how your history shaped you, your beliefs and your behavior, you are in a better position to change anything that you don't particularly like about what you were given.

It may be helpful to take some time to sit down and really think about the messages you may have received from your faith about sex. Answering these questions may help you understand what "stuff" your faith gave you about discussing sex. As not everyone was raised in a family with a strong religious background, these questions won't apply to everyone.

1. **If you were raised in a religious family, what were that religion's beliefs about dating, masturbation, sex, pornography, etc.**

2. **How did your faith share those beliefs with you? Was it direct in sermons, Sunday school, youth group etc? Were the messages implied?**

3. **As a child how did you feel about the messages from the church about sex and sexuality? Were the messages scary? Were the messages given in a manner that you connected with?**

4. **As an adolescent, did you have any conflict between your growing sexual feelings and the teachings of your church? If so, how did you handle these emotional conflicts?**

5. **Have you continued to practice the faith in which you were raised? Why or why not?**

6. **How do you think that your religious upbringing has influenced your thoughts and feelings about talking to your child about sex and sexuality?**

7. **Have you passed the message of shame onto your child?**

After spending time reflecting on the answers to these questions, ask yourself one final question. What did messages did I get about sex and relationships from my your religious upbringing. These messages are often both overt and implied. How then, do these messages influence how I either to or do not talk to my children about sexuality and relationships.

When Sexual Abuse is Involved

Another life experience that can frame our thoughts, feelings and behaviors about sexuality is a history of abuse. Abuse can be physical, sexual, and/or emotional. Though often not thought of, neglect is also a form of abuse. When most people think of abuse, they tend to think of what we call Big T traumas. These are often overt, catastrophic trauma that can include sexual assault, physical assault, being exposed to the ravages of war or even natural disaster.

What most people don't realize is that other trauma, what we call little t trauma, can be just as devastating to a person as a Big T trauma. Trauma and the experience of trauma is very personal. Two people can have the same or a very similar experience and will potentially have very different responses. Depending on many different factors, one person may end up experiencing PTSD symptoms and another may not. Trauma is very individual. Something that you consider traumatic, I might not and vice versa.

I want to start with a proviso about trauma. This book is not meant to address a parent's personal trauma but to discuss how that trauma may affect how he or she handles discussing sex and sexuality with their child. If you have experienced any type of trauma, sexual or otherwise, and experience lasting effects or symptoms of PTSD, it is my strong advice that you seek out the counsel of a therapist who specializes in the treatment of trauma and abuse. There are great modalities for treating trauma for both mind and body. If you are interested in finding out more about some of these trauma treatments, you can look into: EMDR, somatic experiencing, brain spotting or cognitive behavioral therapy for trauma. This can be a very touchy area for many people and it is not my intent to trigger anyone who has a trauma history. However, we need to know how that history can affect how we handle uncomfortable topics such as pornography or sexual education. If you struggle with this topic, please seek out treatment. Though difficult, you will feel better for it in the end.

As a true, in depth discussion of the effects of trauma on sexuality could encompass an entire book (and does for many authors); I will try to sum up my thoughts on the effects of trauma or any kind of our "stuff" about sex. That word is SHAME. The experience of abuse of any kind in childhood, often leaves the abused with core beliefs that there is something wrong with them. Children are not able to process abuse and often take the responsibility or blame for the abuse themselves. Developmentally, depending on the age, children are very "I" focused. Therefore, if Mom or Dad or uncle or some other adult abuses me in some way, it must be my fault. This taking on of blame nearly always means the taking on of shame. There must be something wrong with me. I must be bad. These "less than" messages become internalized and feed the sense of shame.

As we get older, these shame messages stay with us. These messages shape how we interact with the world and particularly with certain topics. Carrying the scars of the abuse nearly always affects adult behavior. In the context of this book, the effects of abuse can vary. The carried shame may make a parent avoid uncomfortable topics all together. As we have seen, sex is an uncomfortable topic to begin with. If talking about sex brings up memories of abuse or is triggering, a parent is likely to avoid the topic all together. If a person internalized his or her abuse and shame with the beliefs that sex is shameful and bad, again, the topic of sex will likely be avoided. If the topic of sex is not avoided, the discussions of sex may be shaming.

This is the type of behavior that continues cycles of shame. If a parent feels shame about sex, they are likely to pass those beliefs on to their children. Children may be taught that sex and sexuality are shameful. In this, we are back to the pattern discussed previously. If I have sexual feelings and I have been taught that sex is shameful and bad, I must be shameful and bad.

This discussion of the effects of abuse on one's willingness to talk about sex and relationships has been simplified. My purpose is not to go into this topic in depth but to let parents know that if they have any abuse history, even if it is not sexual abuse, this history has shaped your core beliefs and can have a profound effect on how you interact with and talk to your children, especially about tough topics like sexuality and relationships.

It may be helpful to take some time to reflect upon your own abuse history. This is painful for many people and often should be done with professional assistance.

1. **Was I abused as a child? Remember, what defines abuse is very personal for everyone. If you feel that you were abused, that is enough to qualify as a yes answer.**

2. **Does this abuse affect my adult behavior?**

3. **Have I ever received professional counseling to help me deal with my abuse?**

4. **Would I benefit from professional help regarding my abuse? Should I seek help?**

5. **How does my abuse history affect how I deal with (or don't deal with) discussions of sex and sexuality with my children?**

I will reiterate my honest desire for anyone who has suffered from sexual abuse, or any other type of abuse in childhood, if they have not already, to seek professional help in order to start their journey to healing.

Up until now, we have talked about things from our family of origin (childhood) that can affect our views and beliefs about sex and relationships and the effect these beliefs have on how a parent talks, or doesn't talk, to their child about sex and relationships. There are, of course, other factors that influence the process that do not stem from our childhoods. Our past is not always to blame.

Sexual Education in the Schools

One factor that studies have shown can influence the parental discussion with a child about sex is education. Some parents do not have enough knowledge about sex, relationships, sexually transmitted diseases, birth control, etc., to adequately answer their children's questions. Additionally, many parents make an assumption that all of these facts are covered in the sexual education courses provided by schools. Most American schools have some form of sex education program. However, these programs vary from state to state.

According to the National Conference of State Legislatures site (updated January 1, 2015), all states are "somehow" involved with the sexual education of their students. The facts about state policies on sexual education are interesting and actually scary in some cases, particularly if parents are relying solely on school to educate children about sex. Here are some facts about state sex education requirements from the NCSL site. There are only 22 states in the United States that require public schools to teach some form of sex education. The District of Columbia also has this requirement. Thirty three states mandate some education about HIV/AIDS. Twenty of the twenty two states that require public schools to teach sex education require education about HIV/AIDS as well. It is disheartening that only 22 states require sex education. It is also curious as to how the other 11 states teach students about HIV/AIDS without also teaching about sex as sexual contact is one way that the disease is spread.

A disheartening fact about the sexual education curriculum in American schools is that only 19 states require the curriculum to be "medically, factually or technically accurate." This fact is incredibly disturbing. Not only do only 22 states require sexual education be taught in school, but only 19 of these states require that what is taught be medically accurate.

American sexual education can be problematic if a parent is relying solely on the school system to teach their child about sex and relationships. These curricula also only broadly mandate sexual education, so only the rather progressive programs will also teach about relationships. If parents are unaware of the school policy on sex education, they may be relying on a school that doesn't teach accurate information. They may be relying on a school that won't teach about disease transmission as well. Another disturbing thought given today's technological world, is that most schools do not include education about pornography, cybersex, sexting and the vast array of possibilities that occur when sexuality and digital technology are combined.

Parents in the US have rights regarding their child's sexual education in school. Many states, 37, allow parents to be involved in the sexual education program and three states require a parent's consent before their child can take the classes. Finally, 35 states as well as the District of Columbia allow a parent to remove their child from the classes or "opt out" on their child's behalf.

If a parent opts their child out of school sexual education programs, one can make several assumptions. First, it is possible that the parent wishes to teach the child about sex and relationships on their own. Often this is done based on religious values and beliefs. Home schooled sex education can be a very positive thing. Parents can be a good source of information for children about sex and relationships and we know from studies that children want more of this information from their parents. However, if the parents who are providing the information have any of the "stuff" talked about earlier in this chapter, the accuracy of the information provided to children may be questionable as well as the detail of the information provided.

Another option that may occur if a parent opts their child out of school sexual education is that they do not talk to their child about sexuality and relationships at all. This is something that I have seen with clients as well. No one teaches them anything about sex and they are left to their own devices to find out what is going on. If a child has no guidance where do they look for information? That information often comes from peers or perhaps pornography. Ignoring a subject doesn't make it go away. Parents who completely ignore talking to their children about these sensitive issues are leaving the door open to potential problems. Avoidance and denial don't make things go away. If you don't talk to your child about sex it doesn't mean that they are not going to have sex. If you don't talk to your child about online pornography, it doesn't mean they will not look at it. It just means that they will engage in sexual activities without education or guidance from their parents. Who would you rather have talk to your child about sex? You or his or her 13 year old peers.

Another concern about sexual education either by the school or the parent, relates back to the premise of this book. Many schools do not teach about digital sexuality, and even fewer parents do. Many parents are not aware of all the ways their children use their technology nor all the ways technology can be used for sexual purposes. If a parent does not have the knowledge, they cannot pass it on to their child. Additionally, if the school's curriculum is out of date or doesn't touch on these subjects, the education is lacking some critical features.

If you are a parent who would like to learn more about sexual education programs that deal with digital sexuality, I suggest looking into Sex Ed in the Digital Age. This is a curriculum developed by Carolyn Cooperman and can be found at the Center for Sex Education. (http://www.sexedstore.com/sex-ed-in-the-digital-age/)

This chapter was not designed to place blame on any one person, family, upbringing, religion, etc. The goal of this chapter is truly self-exploration and self- analysis. It is critical for a parent to understand what they bring to the table in terms of their own history, beliefs and discomfort about sex. Without a true understanding of our own thoughts and beliefs about sex and sexuality how can we address these issues competently and confidently with our children? Sex is a topic loaded with baggage. My clients often come to the realization that their parents did the best that they knew how to do when it came to teaching them about sex and relationships. My hope is that this chapter will help you come to understand what might hold you back in this area and help you communicate in a healthy way with your child about sex. If you come to understand your own history, anxiety or discomfort about sex and work through it, you improve your "best that you can" and foster growth in your relationships and hopefully prevent issues with your child and cybersexuality down the road.

Chapter 6

●●●●●●●●

Don't Be in Denial:
Proactive Discussions
with your Child

How do you talk to your child about sex? Many parents wonder what to say, how to say it and worry if they will mess something up by saying the wrong thing. In my experience, many parents don't actually say anything to their children or they say very little too late. Talking to kids about sex was the topic of a 2014 survey conducted by the United Kingdom company, Lil-Lets.

In September of 2014, Lil-Lets published the results of a survey that asked parents questions related to talking to their children about uncomfortable sex education topics: everything from puberty to menstruation to sex. Unfortunately, the results of this survey line right up with other research findings and what I find in clinical practice. Parents are embarrassed.

The study surveyed 2,000 parents. Sixty percent of these parents stated that they have a hard time talking to their children about sensitive topics. This meant not just talking about sex itself but also the biology of puberty and sexual development. Half of the parents stated that they found talking about these topics embarrassing. Apparently "the talk" causes a great deal of anxiety for parents, some of whom reported worrying about having to have a sex talk with their child from the time their child was around four years old.

A surprising finding from the survey was how disconnected the parents were from each other when it came to talking to their child about sex. Instead of working as a team and parenting together, 41% of the parents reported arguing with each other over which parent was going to talk to their child. Some of the survey participants even stated that they and their spouse had come to blows while arguing about the topic.

Despite all the anxiety and fighting that may go into the preparation for "the talk," more than 50% of parents did eventually talk with their child. The concerning statistic for me and my work is that four in ten parents admitted to completely avoiding talking to their children about sex, relationships and puberty. This is what I often hear from my clients who are struggling with pornography addiction. No one talked to them about sex. They had to rely on school sex education programs and most of those do not talk about pornography, sexting or other digital and current topics.

Parents who do not talk to their children about sex at all are leaving their education up to school, but this education is often supplemented by peers and the Internet. Many of these kids don't get accurate information about sex and relationships from peers and the media.

I was at a conference listening to a man speak on the topic of teens' use of pornography. He described how his kids feel about how he handles discussions about sexuality. "Dad, are we going to talk about this again?" That is because he believes that parents must talk to their children about sexuality, pornography, sexting, etc. OFTEN. He is correct. A one shot discussion with your child is likely not going to be productive. I am also a firm believer that a "lecture" style talk about pornography or sexting is not going to be nearly as productive as an active discussion with your child.

News stories are a great transition into a potentially uncomfortable discussion. As news stories about sexting appear in the news have a discussion about sexting with your child. But keep it a conversation, not a lecture. "Hey, I saw on the news that a few kids from XXXX high school got in trouble for sending naked pictures of a classmate. What do you think about that? Is that something that is going on at your school?"

This is also a great opportunity to come to understand how your child thinks and feels about these types of behaviors without either assuming that he or she engages in them or doesn't understand the consequences of them. Ask questions. Find out from your child if the school has a policy on sexting. Do they know any kids who engage in the practice? Have they ever been sent a picture they did not want? In order to foster a relationship with your child that does not foster shame, first gather your data. Have general conversations about the practices such as sexting. Ask more questions. Be interested. Don't impose your values in these spaces. Just listen! After you come to understand how your child thinks and feels about these things, you may not need to engage in the "lecture" you envisioned in your mind. You may find out that your child has a good head on his or her shoulders and understands the potential benefits and consequences of something like sexting.

Using the media as a discussion primer is a great way to handle things if you haven't had an actual discovery of your child engaging in online sexual behavior.

Teaching Sexual Health Beyond Using Media Examples

Using a "media intervention" can be a great in the moment way to talk to your child about sexting and/or pornography. However, an even better tactic is to proactively talk to your child about sex and sexuality before you find they are engaging in it themselves. In this, I found inspiration from a training session I attended in September 2015 given by Dr. Douglas Braun-Harvey. He is a clinician who works with out- of-control sexual behavior. He introduced me to the World Health Organization (WHO) definition of sexual health. The WHO considers sexual health an inextricable element of human health. They define sexual health as "a state of physical, emotional, mental and social well-being in relation to sexuality; It is not merely the absence of disease, dysfunction or infirmity. Sexual health requires a positive and respectful approach to sexuality and sexual relationships, the possibility of having pleasurable and safe sexual experiences, free of coercion, discrimination and violence. For sexual health to be attained and maintained, the sexual rights of all persons must be respected, protected and fulfilled."

Dr. Braun-Harvey shared that he breaks down sexual health into six sexual rights. These components of sexual health are: protection from STI's, HIV and unwanted pregnancy, consent, non-exploitative, honesty, shared values and pleasure. Though all of these do not directly relate to cybersexuality, most do and all of the components are worth talking to your children about.

The first measure of sexual health, protection from STI's, HIV and unwanted pregnancy are not directly related to cybersex (pornography and sexting). However, I can see a connection in the discussion of these health issues and cybersexuality. The prevention of sexually transmitted diseases is tradition-ally taught in sexual education programs in schools. However, you need to be very aware of what your child's school teaches in relation to sexual health. As we have seen in previous chapters, not all schools in the United States provide sexual health curriculum, and they are not all mandated to actually provide accurate information about sexual health. For long term health and well-be-ing, you need to be able to talk to your child about sexual disease transmission and how they can protect themselves. I realize that this may be against the religious beliefs of some readers. Though I respect a reader's religious beliefs, science tells us that abstinence-only programs do not actually prevent teens from having sex. What it does prevent is obtaining accurate knowledge about sex, pregnancy and disease prevention. Many of the teens who were given abstinence-only education can end up infected with an STI and have no idea of signs or symptoms. They may also be less likely to come forward for treat-ment due to shame or embarrassment as they have acted against the religious teachings.

Some teens will engage in anal sex instead of vaginal intercourse as a means of pregnancy prevention. Though this will, obviously, be an effective way to prevent pregnancy, it is NOT an effective way to prevent disease trans-mission. If we do not provide teens with accurate information, they will seek it among their friends. This allows the urban myths of sexuality to live and be perpetuated. Teens will also turn to the Internet for sexual education material. There is some great and truly accurate information online that can teach teens about sexual health, however there are also sites that are of questionable scientific reliability.

One area in which there is overlap into discussions of pornography use involves safe sex. Most pornography videos and images do not depict the actors engaging in protected sexual acts. In discussing this aspect of sexual health with your child, you can point out that the pornography you know they have watched has not depicted sex that took into consideration the possibility of disease transmission. What your teen has been observing in pornography does not truly represent sex between two participants who, hopefully, would both take measures to protect their health.

Sexual Relations and Consent

A key teaching about sexual health involves the concept of consent. Consent is a critical piece of healthy sexuality. Are both parties truly consenting to the sexual encounter? Many teens, and adults for that matter, have misconceptions about the concept of consent. This can be evidenced by the rates of sexual assault and date rape seen on college campuses. There is a wonderful but disturbing movie called *The Hunting Ground* that details several women's experiences of sexual assault on college campuses. This movie not only shows the difficulties these women had in obtaining support from the college they attended, it also shows the attitudes of many young men and women about consent and sexual assault.

Consent is the most fundamental sexual health principle that should ever be considered. Without a truly consenting sexual encounter, we have sexual abuse. In my work with offenders, we teach the differences between coercion, compliance and consent. On the surface, consent appears to be the easiest concept to grasp. A person can truly only give consent if they are not drunk, unconscious, mentally impaired, asleep, etc. In consent, both parties truly know what is going to happen in the sexual encounter and can give a non-impaired agreement to the encounter.

Compliance is something that we often see in the context of relationships but can see in other encounters. Compliance is truly not consent. A person may comply with a sexual contact if they feel that there is a negative consequence to saying no. For example, a young man or woman may comply with a sexual request from a friend or partner if they feel the other person may break up with them if they do not engage in the sex act. This can also be applicable to sexting. The data show us that there is considerably more pressure on girls to send sexual photographs than there is on boys. In my mind, the taking and sending of these pictures can often be compliance instead of consent. What are the social consequences to the girl for not taking the photos? Does she think that the only way to gain a boy's attention is to send a sext message? Is this truly consent? Is she taking these images because she truly wants to or because she fears the consequences? If it is the latter, then this is compliance, not consent.

The final aspect of this trio is coercion. Coercion normally involves some form of cajoling, talking into or "breaking down" of the other party. Is the person talked into doing something that they don't want to do? Coercion can be something more actively fear provoking such as physical threat, but can also be through verbal manipulation. Coercion is also seen in the sexting realm with one teen talking another into engaging in the behavior, perhaps with social threats as the currency.

The concept of consent is very critical to sexting. The scientific literature tells us that there is a difference between consensual and non-consensual sexting. Consensual sexting is something that normally occurs between two adolescents that are in a relationship together. When sexting occurs in this context, it is a relatively "normal" part of courtship and relationship maintenance. In this truly consensual context, there really isn't anything wrong with the behavior outside of the fact that it leaves the sexter open to non-consensual sexting at a future time.

Non-consensual sexting occurs when an image or video is sent to anyone other than the intended party. This can often be seen in high school sexting scandals when an image or group of images end up being forwarded and sent through a large number of the members of a class. This is non-consensual for several reasons. First, the sender of the original message did not intend for the message to be seen by anyone other than the intended receiver. The second reason that this is non-consensual is that the original receiver did not get permission to send the image and did so often without the knowledge of the original sender.

Any discussion of sexting with your teen must include the concept of consent. Help them understand that any image they send leaves their control the moment it is sent. In the moment, they may feel that they are in love or at least very strongly like the person to whom they sent the image. However, relationships change and there are often social pressures on both parties. These general facts of adolescent life make any sexual imagery sent by a teen susceptible to being passed on to another.

When it comes to discussing consent and pornography, the discussion may depend on the type of pornography that your teen is viewing. Any commercially produced pornography has the consent of both parties. They are being paid by a company to voluntarily engage in these sex acts on screen (we will discuss exploitation later). Commercial pornography involves consent. If your teen is viewing other types of pornography, consent becomes a topic of conversation. For example, voyeurism themed pornography sites often include imagery of another person that is taken without their consent. Inherently, these images are abusive since the person in the image cannot give consent. For example, a site that posts users' "up skirt" videos and photos is posting non-consensual imagery. Many of the women in these videos or images have no idea that someone has taken an "up skirt" image and posted it online in a public forum.

Another type of pornography your teen might have viewed is amateur pornography. These are videos that are taken by two people engaging in sexual acts. These are not commercially produced and frequently uploaded voluntarily to sites by the people in the video. However, some of these are videos that have been taken without the knowledge or consent of both parties and it is frequently impossible to know if both (or all) actors in the imagery have given consent.

A final discussion of consent in pornography involves child pornography. Many images of child pornography are images of child sexual abuse. These images inherently involve abusive situations with minors who cannot give consent. These images are illegal in the United States. If your child is viewing them, there are potentially very serious consequences if caught. If not caught, the child is perpetuating the abuse of the children in these images by viewing the pornography.

The difficulty comes with youth produced sexual imagery. A larger percentage of child pornography that is surfacing lately is youth produced imagery. These images get culled from various sites and posted on other sites online.

There are two ways this happens. The first is that a youth truly, voluntarily creates this imagery to send to, perhaps, a boyfriend or girlfriend. The second way this happens is when children are coerced into taking sexual imagery of themselves by a person they meet online in a chat room or messenger app. The second way is clearly non-consensual. However, even those youths who did voluntarily take sexual imagery of themselves, did not give permission for anyone to take those images and post them anywhere else on the Internet.

If you watch the news or follow stories online, you can see how very necessary it is to have conversations about consent with your children.

Sexual Exploitation

Another key concept to sexual health is that all sexual interactions a person engages in should be non-exploitive. Exploitation can be seen in many aspects of sexuality and also in cybersexuality. Exploitation can be defined as using or manipulating another person for one's own purposes. In the seminar I attended, Douglas Braun-Harvey defined exploitation as leveraging power to gain access to sexual activity.

Exploitation is a concept that can readily be applied to cybersex and pornography. There are some people who feel that any pornography, even that which is professionally produced by paid actors, is exploitative and therefore not okay under any circumstances. The purpose of this book is not to look deeply into this issue but to discuss it in terms of how it applies to talking to your child. Exploitation in pornography can more commonly be seen in non-professionally produced pornography. Any pornography that is posted on a site that is, for example, a revenge pornography site, is both exploitation and non-consensual. The past relationship during which the video was created is being exploited to meet the needs of the person posting the video to the revenge pornography site.

Another cyber avenue for exploitation is the use of webcams and video sites. If teens are experimenting with their sexuality on any of these types of sites, their sexual video imagery can be captured (recorded) by the person on the other end. This imagery can then be used to exploit the teen. This is a tactic sometimes used by adults who are engaging in video sexual contact with a minor. They may, in effect, blackmail the minor with the video content.

Sometimes, the adult will exploit the child by threatening to share the video with parents or peers and will not do so in exchange for continued interaction online.

Exploitation can become apparent when we look at sexting. The leveraging of power doesn't have to be direct from one person but can also be the leverage of peer pressure. As we talked about earlier, when it comes to sexting, there is a difference in the social stigma for girls and boys who engage in the behavior. Girls feel more pressure to engage in sexting and yet are socially seen in a less favorable light when they do sext. This social disparity can be used to the advantage of the person pressuring a teen for a sext. The social system is extremely important to teens. In order to gain the attention of a person who is considered popular or of the right crowd, a girl might feel pressured to send a picture.

Not all sexting is exploitative. Teens who are in a relationship may consensually sext with each other. When you find out your teen is sexting, don't assume they are being exploited, but talk about the dynamics of the relationship that led to the behavior. If it is consensual, then the discussion is about safety and privacy of imagery. If the behavior is exploitative, the conversation will lead in a different direction.

Another aspect of sexual health that fits well into the conversations about cybersexuality and sexting is that of shared values. Everyone has a different set of values by which they live. For some, this is guided by their religion. For others, they have another moral compass that guides their beliefs and actions. Many people have a set of values that do not align with pornography in any fashion nor with sexting. The purpose of this book is not to discuss those religious beliefs or values nor to debate them. Each person has their own. Our goal is to help you talk about these in relation to cybersexuality.

If you and your family hold a religious belief that does not align with pornography and you find your child looking at the imagery, please try to refrain from shaming your child when talking to them. Statements like, "This is a sin," or "God won't be happy with you" are statements that use shame to try to guide behavior as opposed to communication. Shame statements can cause your child to internalize the shame, stigmatize their own sexuality and subvert the behavior into secrets. Addiction and shame live in secrets.

The best way to handle this is with a discussion about why your child is looking at pornography. Perhaps the child is curious about sex and sexuality and is seeking information. Perhaps the child is looking for an outlet for sexual expression. These are all valid and legitimate reasons why teens may seek out online pornography.

This is an opportunity for education. What have they been taught about sex by you or in school? What questions do they still have? Are they having sexual feelings? How can you, as the parent, supplement their sex education in a healthy way that also is in line with your value?

In lieu of shaming your child because his or her behavior is not aligned with your religious faith, the best course of action is to ask them how they feel about it. Many children who also hold their parent's religious values feel a great deal of shame already about looking at pornography, sexting etc. They know that the behavior doesn't mesh with their religion and can feel bad about it. Adding shame to these feelings can cause bigger, longer lasting problems than can occur from viewing pornography itself. Talk to your child about the struggle they may have. How does one reconcile one's behavior with one's religious beliefs? Engaging in a behavior that goes against a religious value does not make a person a bad person, simply human. These moments can not only deepen your communication and connection with your child but may also deepen their understanding of their faith.

For those individuals who are not guided by a specific religious set of values, this can be a great opportunity to talk to your child about your values and to help them learn to define their own. In order to do this, you the parent, must already know your own values about sex and sexuality (see previous chapter if you skipped it). When you know this, you can talk to your child about what shaped your values. How did you come to view pornography as you do now? Find out from your child how they feel about it. Where do these thoughts or feelings come from? What information can you provide your child to help them create and define their own sexual values?

In summary, the bottom line is that you have to talk to your teen about sex and cybersexuality often and early. If you are waiting until your child is 15 or 16 years old, you are too late. Odds are they have at least seen online pornography by that time (average age of first exposure is 11) even if they have not actively searched for it. Start teaching aspects of sexual health early on. The concepts of compliance, coercion and consent are topics that can be applied not only to sexuality but to other social dynamics so can be taught to younger children as well. Use the news and media coverage of sexting events to your advantage. Have the dialogue about the story you saw posted on Facebook or Twitter with your child.

Most importantly, just talk to your child. Don't lecture. Just talk. Have a conversation where you are willing to hear his or her point of view with openness. A key to teaching sexual health to anyone is to talk about sex and sexuality without judgment.

Chapter 7

●●●●●●●●

You've Found Your Child Engaging in Cybersex: Now What?

The first thing I need to say in this situation is "DON'T PANIC." Many parents, if they have not done their own work, (as we discussed in an earlier chapter) get very anxious, panicked, upset or angry when they discover their child is engaging in sexting or looking at pornography online. This is not a moment to panic, this is an opportunity. What you have before you is the opportunity to talk to your child and guide him or her while also learning about them and their world.

Before we get into the "now what?" I want to take a moment to ask a question. When thinking about finding your child sexting or looking about pornography, does the word "caught" come into mind? What if I catch my daughter sending a nude picture? What if I catch my son looking at pornography on his phone? If these are some thoughts you have had, you are not alone.

However, I want us to take a look at the language we use in this case. If you think I am being particular, let me tell you why I am.

When working with my sexually addicted clients, we always talk about what happened if anyone (mostly parents) ever found them looking at pornography or masturbating. The language of "caught" always comes up. Mom caught me masturbating. Dad caught me looking at pornography. The act of being "caught" produced shame and embarrassment in the majority of my clients.

The next thing we always talk about is the reaction of the person who "caught" them. Most of the time the "catcher" was reactive, said something negative or did not respond well. My clients frequently garnered one message from this interaction. Sex is shameful and embarrassing. There must be something wrong with me if I am engaging in this behavior. From that point on, shame has entered their sense of sexuality. If I am ashamed of something, I will keep it secret. Shame and secrets are two of the hallmarks of sexual addiction.

In today's digital world, if we "catch" a teen looking at pornography online, we are "catching" a normative behavior. Viewing pornography for many adolescents is a part of their sexual exploration. Access and availability have made online pornography a venue for sexual exploration and sex education. If we use shaming language with our children or shame them for engaging in something normative, we are fusing sex and shame together. This fusion has the potential to lead to trouble in the future.

The goal of talking to your child is to prevent problematic sexual behavior, not to create it. This is why I am very mindful of the language I use when discussing this matter, as well as the language I use in my mind when I think about it. If I think I have caught someone doing anything this shapes how I may or may not react. If I think that I have found something, it changes the context.

Another thing to think about here is how we find out that the child is engaging in cybersexual behaviors. Our knee jerk response is likely to be very different if we find a pornography site in the cookies of the laptop than if we get a call from the school principal indicating that our child was found to be sending naked pictures of a classmate. One situation has the distinct possibility of ramping up our own issues and anxieties (call from the principal). Regardless of the type of discovery you have, your response should be the same no matter what. CALM.

Before I talk about how to talk to your child, I want to share the work of Carol Dweck and how we use her idea of the growth mindset in treatment. The growth mindset concept also applies here as well. Carol Dweck is a wonderful researcher and author (www.mindsetonline.com) who created the idea of fixed and growth mindsets. This work originated out of her work in educating children, but it has broad applications. A fixed mindset is one in which the person thinks that their qualities are fixed traits. For example, "I am smart" or "I am stupid." If a person thinks that a trait is fixed, they do not think that they can change that trait or behavior. A growth mindset, on the other hand, is one in which the person does not think their abilities are set in stone. In a growth mindset, if something negative has happened, we acknowledge it but also acknowledge that it is over and then try to learn from it and move forward. In our practice we do not dwell on the mistakes in a negative manner but try to use each slip or interaction that didn't go so well as an opportunity to learn and do better the next time.

How does this apply to talking to your child? In my mind, it applies perfectly. If you approach the issue of finding your child looking at online pornography or sexting you can approach it in several ways. If you approach it from a fixed mindset, you may convey a message to your child that there is something wrong with them for engaging in this behavior. They are perhaps a troublemaker, sick, perverted, stupid, shameful or sinful. If you don't say these things to your child but you are thinking these thoughts in your mind, you may convey the message in tone and intonation without having to use the words. These thoughts are fixed mindset traits. If you think that your child is a trouble maker, this is a label that can skew you and your child's thoughts on their ability to change this trait.

If you approach the issue from a growth mindset, you will approach it without labels and potential shame. So you walk into your child's room and see pornography on the screen. To approach this from a growth mindset is to say, "OK, I'm not really excited about this but it is done. My child is looking at pornography. How can I handle this so that we both can learn from the discovery and move forward in a healthy way?" By doing this, you don't shame your child. You are also instilling in them the idea that communicating about difficult issues is not only possible but is a good thing. You will both learn from such a conversation.

Having "the Conversation"

So how do you actually have the conversation? Here I am going to borrow some fabulous advice from the book, *Crucial Conversations*, written by Joseph Grenny, Kerry Patterson and Ron McMillan. This book is full of amazing tips and tools to help you successfully have hard conversations. I am going to pull a few of their tips into our topic, talking to your child about your discovery of their sexual behavior.

The first tip they give that I think is paramount to any conversation is to create safety. If there is not an air of safety between the people in the discussion, it will likely not occur without moving into what the authors call silence or violence. This means the discussion will likely end up in a fight or in stone cold silence. One way to make sure that the environment for the conversation is safe is to not have the conversation before you have checked in with your own emotions. Is your anger in check? Is your panic in check? Have you processed this with your spouse, the other parent of the child, a trusted friend or family member? Can you have the conversation calmly? If not, you are jumping ahead of yourself and possibly going to send shaming messages to your child if you try to talk to them now. If you are still sitting in your emotions and reactive, you are likely not going to be able to start the conversation and send the message of safety to your child.

If you have checked in with your own feelings and can be the adult in the conversation, you are more likely to be able to create safety. This is the time to have the discussion.

How should the conversation go? Here, I will turn again to a tip from the *Crucial Conversations* book. State the facts. Avoid getting into your story or the story you have made up in your mind. Simply put, state why you are having the conversation. "I was on the computer and saw that you were looking at a pornography website." "I was using the tablet and saw pornography in the search history." Before you get into your story (the things you are making up in your mind), simply ask your child for the facts. Be present and in the moment.

As a therapist, I am a proponent of both honesty and naming what is going on in a situation. A conversation about pornography with your child is going to be as uncomfortable for you as it is for him or her. On the outside, no teen really wants to talk to mom or dad about sex or pornography, particularly when you know what they have been looking at. I like to start conversations by naming my emotions. For example, "I know this is going to be uncomfortable for both of us but it is something we have to talk about. I was on the computer and saw that you were looking at pornography sites and I want to talk to you about it."

In order to not shame your child, it is critical that you understand and express that you do get that today's children engage in their sexual exploration online.

In being honest, you may have to own that you may not have all the answers. I would absolutely suggest that you ask more questions than lecture. How did they learn about online pornography? Why do they look at it? Do they have any questions about sex? How do they feel about the videos or images they see? Do they think that watching pornography is a problem? How does it mesh with your family's religious beliefs? Are these images such that you are comfortable having them on what may be a shared computer in the house? What views of sex and sexuality are they getting from the videos?

The above is a list of many questions--and there are many more. What becomes obvious from this list is the fact that this is not a one-time conversation. Gathering your data about your child's pornography use is going to take more than one calm conversation. It is going to require that you both engage in the awkward conversations until they no longer become awkward.

In this moment, I am reminded of a conversation with a fellow sex addiction therapist that I had at a conference. She is a single mother to two teenage boys. She found that her oldest son was watching pornography and masturbating. In good therapist fashion, she sat down and talked to him about it. They even sat and watched the pornography video together. This prompted an awkward (for him) moment but a great conversation about objectification of women in pornography and the fact that in most pornography, there is nothing relational. It is all performance based sex. Her request, owning that her son was in the midst of discovering his burgeoning sexuality, was that when he masturbate, he do so without pornography. This too, prompted a very good conversation about the desensitization that occurs with large amounts of pornography use and how that could affect his sexuality and sexual performance.

In the case of a sexting discovery, things may be a bit more volatile or reactive as, depending on the mode of discovery, there may be legal or school consequences on hand. In these situations, it is even more important that a parent processes their emotions first, prior to the discussion. If you are very reactive there will be no safety. Being reactive in this situation is, of course, very understandable. If you are dealing with this, it is serious. However, calmer heads need to prevail. Safety has to be paramount or else a situation like this can easily escalate to fights and accusations.

Again, start with facts. "The Principal just called me and told me that several students were found with naked pictures on their phones, and you are one of the students. I am really concerned about this and want to find out from you what is going on before I jump to any conclusions." These types of issues, with potential long-term consequences, are going to require many conversations and a large amount of fact gathering. The first conversation, perhaps, is gathering the facts from your child as to what happened. Did they possess, receive, or send a picture? Was the picture of them? Who did they send it to? What is your child's understanding of what will happen next?

Other conversations are going to require more facts. First, what is going to happen due to the sexting discovery? Is someone going to the police and will files be charged? Is the school handling this in a disciplinary fashion? What do you need to do to help your child? For example, do they need an attorney? Do they need to see a therapist for assessment or treatment?

Gather your facts before you have conversations and make plans. It is best to include your child in on these plans and fact gathering assignments as well. They need to see and be part of the consequences of their actions. However, it is also critical that they see and feel that you are supporting them. You don't have to agree with what your child has done to support them. You don't have to be happy with them to support them, but you do need to support them emotionally through the process. In this you are not only modeling healthy communication and crisis management but also unconditional love.

As you can see, there is no true prescription for talking to your child about sex, cybersex or sexting. What is very obvious is that it is always easier to have a proactive conversation than a reactive conversation. If you have spent the time talking to your child proactively about these issues, it is less likely that you will end up having a traumatic discovery of their behavior. However, even if you have had good discussions about sex, pornography and sexting with your child, you may still find yourself in the position of having a reactive conversation.

Key points to remember are to create safety for your child in the conversation. If your child feels safe talking to you, they are less likely to lie or stonewall and more likely to have a real (though maybe stunted) conversation with you about the issue. As the parent and the adult, it is our responsibility to model healthy communication as well as healthy problem solving. Your child will learn more from what you model in your own behavior than from what you say.

Chapter 8
●●●●●●●●

How Do I Know If My Child's Online Sexual Behavior is a Problem?

The issue of what is problematic is problematic itself. Behavior that may be a problem for the parent may not, in fact, be problematic, in the clinical sense, for the child. As I write this, I am reminded of an adolescent client that we had at the office. The parents wanted the child assessed to see if he had a pornography addiction or some other type of problematic sexual behavior. The mother had found that her son was looking at pornography online. She brought it to his educational therapist and she suggested a referral. In treatment, it was determined that the teenage boy had looked at and occasionally did watch pornography online. His pornography viewing was not getting in the way of his functioning. He was maintaining good grades. He had a rich and active social life. He was active in school sports and was not getting in trouble in any way in the family. As an expression of his sexuality, he did sometimes view and masturbate to online pornography.

In further sessions with the family, it turned out that the fact that the teenage boy was looking at pornography was not the true issue for the mother (dad saw no issue at all). What the mother objected to was the content of the pornography he was watching. This young man was not watching violent pornography, rape pornography or even any type of fetish pornography. The young man had a preference for a female body type that was not within the social norm. This "out of the box" arousal template was what the mother had a concern with, not the fact that her son was watching pornography.

This case is a great example of us, the parent or adult, putting our own sexual beliefs on the child and expecting them to conform. It was difficult for her to see that her son didn't have a problem with pornography despite the fact that his preference was for a non-traditional body type. It wasn't "normal" to her and she had a hard time accepting it. This is not meant to be a judgment on this well-meaning and good mother who did the right thing and sought professional help to determine if her son had a problem. It is, however, an example of how a parent's own sexual ideas, thoughts and issues can cloud discussions of sexuality with their child.

Clinical Definition of Pornography Nonexistent So Far

In the truest clinical sense, there is no such thing as a problem with pornography or pornography addiction. When I say this, I am referring to the view of the American Psychiatric Association, who are the publishers of the Diagnostic and Statistical Manual, currently in its 5th edition. The APA is also responsible for determining what is and what is not a psychiatric condition. The most recent edition was published in 2015, and despite some effort from those of us who work in the sexual addiction field, pornography addiction was not included in the newest edition. A lack of empirical evidence was cited for its lack of inclusion and lack of inclusion in the appendix. This conclusion was made despite a growing body of evidence supporting compulsive sexuality and inclusion of other behavioral addictions such as gambling.

I briefly delve into this in order to provide some background. There is a great divide in American culture about sexual addiction or pornography addiction. We wonder if it exists or is it a made up problem created by sexually conservative clinicians who are trying to make money treating people who watch pornography. The idea of sexual addiction and compulsivity are currently in the same position that alcoholism found itself in the early 1900's. It is either seen as a moral failing by society or, on the opposite side, the oppression of a person's right to sexual expression.

Those of us who work in the field truly understand that Internet pornography can be addictive. Its compulsive use can create extreme and intense problems in the lives of users and it can destroy families. On a practical level, for someone who is either a pornography addict or the family member of a pornography addict, the DSM argument doesn't have much of an effect, but for one. If a disorder is not recognized in the DSM-V, your insurance company will NOT pay for treatment for the disorder. If it is not in the DSM, it "does not exist." This means that the majority of people who treat pornography addiction will be out of network and you will have to pay out of pocket.

Is Your Child Addicted?

When trying to ascertain whether or not pornography use is problematic for your child we can assess using some of the same criteria that we use for determining if substance abuse is a problem for a person. How do we do that? We look at how the use of the substance, or in this case pornography or sexting, affects the life of the person who is engaging in the behavior. There are several hallmarks of problematic use that we can assess. We will look at each of these hallmarks and apply them to the problematic use of cybersex.

One of the first hallmarks of problematic use or addiction is tolerance. With substance use, tolerance involves needing more and more of a substance to achieve the desired feeling. For example, a person with an alcohol problem may start drinking a few drinks a night. Soon, their body becomes tolerant to the alcohol and they need to drink more, say a six pack where a few beers used to do, in order to achieve the same buzzed feeling. Over time and repeated drinking, the alcoholic then needs to consume more and more alcohol in order to get a buzz. This is how someone goes from drinking a few beers a night to a fifth of vodka and a case of beer. With alcohol and other substances, there is often a physiological tolerance to the substance that helps this process along.

How does the tolerance process apply to online pornography? The process is very similar. What we know from research is that the dopamine reward system is involved with sex as well as drugs. A similar process occurs in the brain of a pornography user that happens in the brain of a drug addict. The first time a person watches Internet pornography, their brain will get a dopamine "hit". This is completely natural. We are humans and biologically programmed to respond to sexuality. If we didn't have sexual feelings and urges, we would not reproduce and that would be the end of the human race.

For some people, the next time they look at Internet pornography, they may not get the same feeling. They may get a dopamine hit but not as big as the first time. If they want to find that feeling again with the pornography, they have to find other or more material. Many of my clients describe this process similarly. They look at some traditional pornography (say normative heterosexual pornography) and they get a hit the first few times. After that, they don't get the same feeling. Therefore, they start to click their way through the universe of Internet pornography. The content often escalates as a consequence of the tolerance. They may start to look at things like pornography of anal sex, threesomes, bestiality, same sex interactions, fetishes, and sadomasochism. In order for them to find the same "zing" (my very non-clinical term for the feeling) they needed to watch pornography with increasingly taboo themes. For many of my clients, these were things that they were initially interested in but over time were then attracted to viewing.

For some, tolerance does not necessarily manifest in increasingly taboo pornography themes, but in increasing amounts of time spent in the hunt for the perfect image. Another hallmark of addiction is use over longer periods of time than intended. Again, many clients describe this process similarly. Over time and repeated pornography use, they cannot achieve the same feeling they originally did. They will then spend more and more time online hunting for the "perfect" image that will give them the state of arousal and dopamine hit they are seeking. The problem with this is that the "perfect" image or video doesn't exist and they can spend hours and hours online surfing for this image. If they intended to only spend an hour or so online, they may look up from the computer and find that anywhere from two to eight hours have passed. The process of searching or hunting can, in the end, create the same dopamine hit that the images did in the beginning. Many of my clients have told me that in their hunt for this illusive image, they found the end of the Internet.

How can this apply to your child? Instead of just thinking that the presence of pornography itself is problematic, talk to your child about their use of it. How long do they spend online looking at pornography? What types of images do they look at? Has the topic or theme of the pornography escalated since they started to look at online pornography? If the answer to these questions is no, it is possible that your teen does not have a problem with pornography use and his or her use is in the "normal" range. If they report any of these escalations that arise as a result of tolerance, their use may be problematic. Again, a reminder, we are talking about problematic in a clinical sense and not based on moral or religious beliefs.

Another sign of problematic use of either a substance or a behavior is past unsuccessful attempts to stop either using the substance or engaging in the behavior. Many people in recovery from pornography addiction will report trying to stop using pornography many times. Frequently these attempts are unsuccessful in the long term. They may be able to stop for a few weeks or a few months, but those individuals for whom online pornography is truly problematic almost always find themselves returning to it despite their best efforts and sincere desire to stop. They will frequently purge their computer files and delete any pornography they have stored on their computer. They may close accounts on chat sites or webcam sites. They may stop using chat apps like Whisper and Kik. These pauses in behavior are often stressful because they are not getting the help and support they need to improve their chances of recovery. Ultimately, every return to pornography or chat use after a determination to stop brings with it great feelings of guilt, shame and failure.

Whether or not your child has tried to stop their online pornography use or sex chatting is something you will only find out if you ask. If they have had unsuccessful attempts to stop, talk to them about what happened when they tried to stop. This may be one of your biggest indicators of a problem. If your child has not ever tried to stop, also ask about this. Their lack of attempts to stop may indicate a few things. First, it will likely indicate that they don't think they have a problem with the sex chatting or pornography use and there has been no reason to stop. This is fully possible. Not everyone who sex chats or looks at pornography develops an addiction to the behavior. Your child may be able to engage in cybersexuality in a manner that does not cause any problems.

The other side of that coin is that your child's lack of attempts to stop may indicate that they are so sucked in that the thought never crossed their minds, or they may have had the thought to stop but never actually tried to stop. With clients who are not sure if their pornography use is problematic, I often suggest an experiment. We determine an amount of time that the client is willing to go without using any form of cybersexuality (i.e., pornography, chatting, webcam, etc). If they can successfully go this amount of time, usually anywhere from a week to a month, then, chances are, they may not have a problem with the behavior. If, however, the client cannot go a week or two without watching pornography, they likely do have a problem with the behavior. Additionally, if they do make the abstinence goal but the emotional process along the way is very difficult, that may indicate some level of problem as well.

If you and your child are unsure if their cybersex use is problematic, I suggest using this experiment as well. Talk to your child and determine between you a preassigned length of time that he or she will go without engaging in any cybersex activities. At the end of the time frame, if not during the time frame as well, check in with your child about their experience. If all was well, then, from a clinical sense, there is a lower probability that your child has a problem with cybersex. If this is not the case, your child may describe feeling a lot of cravings or urges to engage in the behavior. They may describe the desire to go online and chat in a sexual manner or watch online pornography to relieve boredom or stress from school, etc. If your child talks about any of these or similar issues, it is suggested that they see a professional who specializes in treating pornography addiction for further assessment.

Withdrawal Symptoms

The discussion of attempts to stop or inability to stop leads us directly into the concept of withdrawal. When people think of withdrawal, the most poignant image that comes to mind is that of the withdrawal from heroin addiction. Among drug withdrawals, heroin withdrawal is one of the most painful and obvious (though not deadly like withdrawal from alcohol and benzodiazepines). The concept of withdrawal from pornography is hotly debated as well. Those who support the idea that the behavior is an addiction look to the fact that the chronic compulsive use of sexuality alters the brain's neurochemistry as support for withdrawal. If we stop continuously supplying the substance or behavior, there are going to be changes to the brain neurochemistry and thus changes to behavior as a result. My clients often report that, during their initial time without cybersex, they are not as mentally sharp or acute. Many are a bit grumpy and their fuse is shorter. Many also report some memory issues. Most problematic users will report that stopping the behavior results in many urges and cravings to use pornography.

Some of the best anecdotal support for the withdrawal from digital tech comes from reports of teens (and some adults) who are compulsive Internet users or gamers. If you deny them access to their technology (computer, laptop, tablet, phone, game system, etc), you can quickly see a behavioral meltdown. Many of these teens cannot handle life without their technology. In writing this I am reminded of a young man that I worked with several years ago. He was not only engaging in problematic sexual behavior online, he was a compulsive gamer and Internet user. When his mother would take away his access to his technology or shut down his ability to use social media or YouTube, he could not emotionally handle the withdrawal. He would get angry and agitated. He would have tantrums that you would traditionally see in a toddler and not a teenager. He would emotionally shut down.

Whether or not withdrawal from sexual behavior or technology is real is an argument I will leave to the scientists. What I am more concerned with is what happens in the real world, working with clients. If your child has physical or emotional difficulties when they are not allowed access to cybersex, likely this is a sign of a problem.

Other Hallmarks of Addiction

There are several more hallmarks of addictive behavior. One of them is continued use despite the knowledge of potentially damaging consequences. For example, the person who continues to use drugs or drink despite the fact that their spouse has told them they will file for divorce if they don't stop. The individual thinks: I know that if I continue to drink, my husband will divorce me and I won't be able to see my children. However, I continue to drink, despite not wanting my marriage to end.

Frequently, addicts engage in behaviors that they know are wrong, dangerous, cause emotional pain and suffering to others or are illegal. When their good judgment is overrun by the desire to engage in the behavior (drugs, alcohol, porn, etc) this is a clear sign of problematic use or addiction.

When applying this concept to teens, we have to take some things into account. There is a lack of forward thinking and impulse control that comes with being an adolescent. This impedes the thinking process in and of itself. I think a clear example of this can be seen in accounts of adolescents and sexting. An adolescent would have to be completely unaware to not have ever heard of a sexting scandal or of someone similar to them who has gotten in legal trouble over sexting. These accounts are all over the news. However, many teens still engage in the behavior. They know that they could get in trouble but continue to sext.

When it comes to behaviors like sexting and online pornography use, there are other factors that come into play. A big part of what allows people to act outside their moral values online is the concept of anonymity. This is key, particularly for behaviors such as watching images of child sexual abuse, web chat sites like Chatroullette and messaging on apps such as Kik. The user is behind a keyboard. They can be anyone they want to be. They are anonymous and that anonymity gives some people a feeling of security.

Along with that sense of anonymity comes a sense of "not me." I remember Not Me from the old Family Circus cartoons, but this Not Me is different. This Not Me comes into play when not just adolescents but also adults think about their online sexual behavior. Some kids at another school may have gotten in trouble for sexting but it won't happen to me. My friends wouldn't do that to me or I am only sharing naked images with my boyfriend so those kids in Ohio were in a totally different circumstance than me. I can't tell you how many times clients have told me that they saw someone in the news getting in trouble, often big trouble, for their sexual behaviors online and my client thought to themselves, that won't be me. There is a level of denial in many of the people engaging in online sexual behavior. Revenge porn, arrests and public embarrassment are all possible, but IT WON'T HAPPEN TO ME.

The final addiction hallmark is, to me, one of the key signs of problematic behavior in almost anyone, but most certainly children or teens. This criterion of addiction is as follows: important social, occupational (read school for children) or recreational activities are given up or reduced due to use. This, again, is traditionally for substance abuse but we can apply this to online pornography and sex chat, etc. With children, these things are often clear markers that something is going on with your child. These are the overt behavior changes that can indicate that your child is struggling. That struggle could be depression, bullying, substance issues or cybersex issues as well.

If you know that your child is looking at online pornography or has looked at online pornography, take some time to assess this use through the lens of daily functioning. For example, does your child's pornography use get in the way of his or her school work? Given the fact that the computer is used to do most work in today's age, this is the perfect place for pornography use to interfere. Is your child looking at pornography instead of working on a paper or project? Is the time that they take to do their homework greatly increased due to interspersing pornography viewing with homework? Are they getting sucked into pornography or chat and not doing homework at all or not finishing projects in a timely manner?

If the answer is yes to any of these, then you will need to further assess. Is this a problem of simple distractibility or is it a problem with online sexual behavior? Will targeted attention or time management skills or interventions stop the problem? If so, then this may not be problematic sexual behavior but a lack of time management or attention and focusing skills. If they do not resolve the issue, then your child may be using pornography or online chat in a way that is greatly interfering with his occupation, which at this age, is to be a student.

Another concern is whether use is getting in the way of or hampering your child's social life. This is a hard call for those of us who are digital immigrants and not digital natives. A digital native's social life is online. Online interactions are a vital and integral component of how adolescents socialize today. We have to take this into account.

Things to look for here are changes to behavior. If your child had a core group of friends and no longer spends time with them or spends less time with them, this should be a red flag. The red flag means that something is going on, which is not always related to cybersex. It could be bullying, mental health issues or other social dynamics going on in your child's world. However, if they are not engaging with friends at all in real time or if this is greatly decreased, it is best to investigate, as this could be a sign of a problematic Internet use in general or of problematic cybersex use.

Another rather obvious marker in adolescents involves their activities. Children in today's world are very frequently over booked and involved in many activities. This enormous amount of social and recreational busyness is what makes this a good marker for change. If your child has traditionally engaged in a number of different sports and all of a sudden wants to stop, this is a red flag. If they stop participating in social activities, this is a red flag. If your once active and social child becomes a child who wants to be at home, alone and not engaging, something is wrong.

These social and occupational markers of potential addiction issues are truly markers of some type of distress in your child. One alternative is that they are having an addictive struggle, perhaps with substances or sex. However, there are many other reasons they might be changing behavior. The social landscape of adolescents is very difficult to traverse. Children are subject to bullying by peers which can manifest with the same behavioral changes. They can be subject to peer pressure, pressure to perform in sports or academics that can lead to depression and anxiety. If your child starts to change in any of the above ways, don't jump to an addiction conclusion. Talk to your child to find out what is truly causing the changes. One option may be addiction, but remember there are many other options.

This chapter has provided many ways in which cybersex can be problematic for your child as well as things to look for in their behavior. I want to reiterate that in this chapter we are talking about problematic versus non-problematic in a clinical sense. Does their use interrupt functioning to the point that it is a problem or are they interacting with sexuality in a way that is problematic for them? The determination of a clinical problem is devoid of moral or religious judgment. It is simply looking at whether or not the behavior is impairing functioning.

We don't know what makes one person able to engage with a substance or engage in a behavior such as online pornography without becoming addicted while another similar person does become addicted. This is perhaps a combination of genes and environment, such as early exposure. However, what we do know is that some people can sex chat, web cam and look at online pornography and never have a clinical problem. Other people cannot.

This clinical definition of problem is not to take away from a person's subjective experience of problematic use. A person who views pornography may not have a problem with pornography in a clinical sense. He or she may not experience symptoms such as tolerance or escalation. They many not fit the clinical definition of problematic use. However, for some people, their use of cybersex in any form may go against their own personal values or their religious values. If this is the case, though we may not call it a clinical problem, it is still a problem for the person and needs to be treated accordingly. Therefore, your child may not have a clinical problem with cybersex but their use may create emotional unrest due to the disconnect between his or her values and behavior. We should do everything we can to help this child live a life in line with their personal values.

Chapter 9

●●●●●●●●

What Can a Parent Do?
Tangible Tools for Prevention

Thus far we have spent a lot of time talking about both the normalcy of cybersex and the effects of online sexual content on developing minds. We have also spent a good deal of time talking about talking to your child about sexuality, sexting, pornography and cybersex. Many parents do not feel that this is enough. They want to do more or do something more hands on to try to protect their child from accessing sexual imagery online.

For the purposes of this book, I am not going to talk about and review every type of parental control software that exists. There are fabulous technology bloggers and consumer pages that can do that for you. If you want to check out software brands and reviews you can simply do an Internet search for parental control software and you will find links galore to study. These will be both from manufacturers as well as from review sites such as toptenreviews. com. Additionally, many phones and tablets have controls available in the settings that allow you to limit content both generally and specifically. Also, operating system software, depending on what you use, may also provide free access to parental controls.

Filtering Digital Exposure Via Direct Intervention

Before we get into specifics, this question must be asked: To filter or not to filter. The answer to this truly depends on your personal desire and philosophies. However, there are pros and cons to both sides of the argument. This first thing to acknowledge is that no filter is fool proof. The only way to make sure your child does not ever see any online sexuality is to prevent them from ever being online. This is not a realistic approach in today's world. If you choose to filter you must realize that you cannot simply put a filter on a piece of technology and not think about it again.

The first issue is the amount of technology that children today possess. If you are going to filter, you need to make sure that every piece of Internet enabled technology your child owns has some type of filter or control on it. This means that you have to really think about how many pieces of tech your child owns that can access the internet. The obvious answers here are laptops, PCs, phones and tablets. If you are choosing to use parental filters you need to make sure each and every one of these is locked down. The next thing to think about is gaming devices. Nearly every newer gaming device has Internet access since many of the popular games are interactive. This means that both hand held devices and larger consoles need to be filtered and managed.

If you choose to use filters to block your child's access to adult Internet content on their devices and at home, there are other things to think about as well. You can block your child's access to adult content but you have no control over how his or her friend's parents handle things. In the days before the Internet, teens were often exposed to pornography magazines through their peers. Someone found Dad's or Uncle's *Playboy* and the neighborhood teens would check it out. Based on the imagery easily accessible today, the images in a *Playboy* forty years ago seem rather innocuous, but the concept is the same. Adolescents will show their friends things on their phones which can become the digital native version of "hey, look what I found." It is naive to think that blocking your child's access on their own devices will protect them from ever seeing the images online.

If you choose to use filters, you also have to spend some time carefully thinking about what you are going to block. Let's say you choose the parental control settings on your child's phone to not allow adult content. Okay, so on that particular phone your child cannot access online pornography. What about messaging apps? They can still sext with their friends or significant other. They may still be able to get on live webcam chat apps. They may be able to access videos on YouTube that you would not want them to see as well.

Choosing the filter-only option requires a parent to be continuously learning about the new apps content online. You will have to keep up with how adolescents use technology. You are likely going to have to do a lot more than simply use parental controls. In particular, in order to protect your child from this content, you are also going to have to block their ability to add and delete apps from their phones and tablets. If you do not do this, your child will be able to download one of the multiple apps that mask what apps are on their phone and let them access content you might not like in secret. If you are not tech savvy, you won't have a clue what is going on until you read some newspaper article about it. Choosing a filter-only option likely means that you are going to forever be playing catch up with your child, who is probably more tech savvy and more "in the know" than you are.

Another issue to think about is that "where there is a will, there is a way." Blocking software works on the devices that are blocked, until the person being blocked finds a way around it. In all of my years of working with sex addicts, I have never had anyone put blocking or filtering software on a device who then didn't "test" the software. Call it a test, just making sure it works, or trying to get around it, this is nearly a guarantee. For the addicts I work with, the software blocks their ability to go to their preferred "acting out" sites, but it does not stop the desire to act out. Therefore, in the beginning of recovery, they will try to find a way around whatever software is loaded on the computer, phone, etc. For many, this is a successful attempt as it is nearly impossible to block every single avenue to obtain sexual material online.

For others, the blocking software becomes a challenge. The desire to get around the blocking software is fueled not necessarily by the desire to look at sexual material online but the desire to do something they are told not to do. This type of little rebellion is also commonly seen in addicts who have had restricted access to the Internet and particularly by teens whose parents have put them on some type of Internet lock down. As soon as a new type of blocking software comes out into the marketplace, there are YouTube videos posted online about how to get around the software. This can be something as simple as rebooting your cellphone or installing a system upgrade. Sometimes the software stops working for these reasons and the person being blocked doesn't know it for some period of time. Just know that for some people, the challenge is too much to resist.

When discussing the filter-only option, I am reminded of a young man we worked with several years ago. As a young teen, his parents opted for a filter-only philosophy regarding adult online content. Unfortunately, they only filtered and never really talked to their son about sex, sexuality and online sexual content. Upon meeting the family, the mother of this teen truly thought that her son, who was about 15 when he came to treatment, had never seen online pornography. When she told us this, we knew that she was wrong. Years of doing this work has shown us that there is no way a 15year- old had never seen any sexual imagery online. For those of you who might call me cynical, I will respectfully disagree and call it realistic. This mother was doing the right thing for her children and, in her mind, that was enough. The truth of the matter was that her children had never seen online sexual imagery in their home or on any of the devices that she monitored. So, in that, she was successful. However, when there are young hormones and a will, there is a way. The reality was that this adolescent was viewing online pornography but had to get creative in gaining access. He and his younger brother would go online at retail stores that sold computers. If a model computer was out on display and had Internet access, they would go online in the store and look at online pornography there, in public, on the computer set out for display.

I share this story not to try to shame this parent. She was doing everything she thought she could do and was doing the right thing for her family. I share this story as a cautionary tale. There is no way on earth that a parent can fully block their child's access to adult sexual content online. You can block your child's personal access, in your home, on devices you manage. You cannot ensure that he or she will never access the material on a friend's device, in a store, or in some other way that we adults don't think of. If you choose a block/filter-only option, you must be aware of this fact. Do not block and then think that your work is done. You must also constantly be learning about new technology and apps. You must also talk to your child about how to manage content on the devices of their friends. We cannot block and forget about it. Even blocking is not fool proof.

Pushing Boundaries: What's a Parent to Do?

After writing the above cautions about the filtering option, I feel a bit cynical. However, I reiterate the fact that the cautions above are realistic. Adolescence is a time to push limits and boundaries. It is a time when impulse control is low and curiosity and sensation seeking and risk taking are high. A recent study in the *Journal of Early Adolescence* reported the results of a study that looked at the relationship between the adolescent boys' exposure to Internet pornography in relation to puberty and sensation seeking. This study reported an integrative path model in which pubertal timing (when a boy entered puberty, i.e., early, average or late) and sensation seeking predicted use of Internet pornography. When boys enter puberty, they tend to engage in more sensation seeking behaviors and also start to express sexual curiosity. The boys in the study who were in a more advanced stage of puberty than their peers were more likely to visit sexually explicit websites. The study also found that the more boys viewed sexually explicit content online, the lower their academic performance.

The take home point in this study and in telling you about all the ways a teen (or adult) can get around blocking and filtering software is not to discourage you from using the programs. The decision to block or filter your child's content is a very personal one that every parent or family must make for themselves. The point that I will continue to hammer home to you is that blocking alone is not enough. Even if you think that your child is a "good kid" and won't try to get around the software, the chances are that they will. This doesn't mean that they are, in fact, not a good kid. It simply means that they are a kid. Being a teenager is not a judgment on their moral character or your parenting. Pushing boundaries is something that adolescents simply do as a matter of course. The more grounded in reality you are, the better equipped you will be to handle the situation.

So what else can a parent do? To answer this I will turn to the research of Dr. Wisniewski. Dr. Wisniewski is currently a post-doctoral fellow at Penn State

University. Her area of research and specialization is in adolescent online safety and Internet use. She has also studied this from a family systems approach, looking at the influence of parental styles on how children interact with the Internet and social networks.

Dr. Wisniewski has broken down Internet parenting strategies into what she calls direct parental intervention and active mediation. Direct Parental intervention involves a parent using parental controls and/or reading and setting up a teen's social media privacy settings. This direct intervention is done nearly completely by the parent with little or no input from the child. Active mediation involves parents talking to their teenage children about the content that they post. In active mediation, parents will review the information a teen posts and perhaps comment or respond to post made on a social network site like Facebook or Instagram. It should be noted that Dr. Wiskniewski's work does not solely focus on sexual content online but also on what private information (phone, address, etc.) that a teen gives to others online.

Direct parental intervention is the Internet parenting style we have been talking about up to this point in this chapter. Research has shown that explicit parental restrictions against giving out private and personal information online have actually been associated with the increased likelihood that a teen will give out this information online. Remember that boundary pushing, risk taking and lack of impulse control is common in teens. Research has also shown that parental mediation strategies are not very effective in reducing the risk exposure a teen has online, be that pornography, violence or privacy risk behaviors.

Parents who directly mediate their child's behavior online may prevent them from engaging in risky behavior. However, there is a side effect of this restriction. Children don't learn from their mistakes and don't learn how to successfully navigate a risky online world. The teens who are exposed to some risk online learn better coping skills and resilience. This resilience has been found to be a mediating factor in whether or not a child is harmed by exposure to online pornography, bullying, etc. Dr. Wisniewski's studies have found that teens who have parents who are actively engaged in their online world, but are not too restrictive, exhibit higher levels of moral judgment about their online behavior.

Dr. Wisniewski and her colleagues have created Internet parenting profiles based on her work. The first parenting profile is the unengaged parent. This parent is low on direct intervention and low on active mediation. In non-research terms, this parent is either in denial about their child's Internet use, is too busy to pay attention to what they are doing online or is extremely permissive in their parenting style. The second profile is the controlling parent. This parent his high on direct intervention and low on active mediation. This means that a controlling parent simply blocks and filters everything and really doesn't talk to their child about online privacy or online risk. They block it and are done with it. The third profile is the counseling parent. This parent is low on direct intervention and high on active mediation. A parent with this style is likely not using any type of blocking or filtering software. They are, however, talking to their child about online risk and exposure as well as interacting with them online and discussing their content. The final parenting category is the highly engaged parent. This parent is high on both direct intervention as well as high on active mediation. This parent does block content that they feel is age inappropriate for their child. However, they also talk to their child about online risk frequently and interact with them in their online world.

So what is the best Internet parenting style to use? According to current research, the highly engaged parenting style may be the best style to use in order to mitigate your teen's online risk. This allows you to reduce some exposure to risk while also allowing them to engage with peers online in a meaningful manner. The author suggests that new designs for parental monitoring software are called for that helps parents engage in conversations with their teen about the online risk taking behavior instead of simply blocking their risk. We need to not only talk to teens but help them learn the healthy coping styles that will make them more resilient. This resilience will help them not only to deal with online risk but also to deal with any other difficulties that emerge in their lives.

Chapter 10

●●●●●●●●

Resources for Parents

S o how do parents keep up with the rapidly changing and moving world of teen technology? There are lots of resources out there that can help you gather data about your child's digital world. This chapter will provide you with a sampling of all of the resources that are available to assist you in this journey. In no way will this be a comprehensive list. First, there is just too much out there on the Internet to cover everything. Second, things change on a daily basis. As soon as I can compile a good list for this chapter, it will be outdated and more data will emerge. This will serve as a smattering of resources at the time of this writing.

Websites for general information

1. **Connectsafely.org.** The company that runs this website is a non-profit organization that is based in California's Silicon Valley. The site was founded by a technology journalist named Larry Magid. This site

provides new information, safety tips and guides for parents to help them navigate the ever changing digital world as well as to help them learn how to connect online in a safe manner. The organization hosts Safer Internet Day, which is a day of awareness that in 2016 was held on February 9. The day also involves a livestream event. The Connectsafely organization also hosts the site One Good Thing. (onegoodthing.org). This site is a "good news" type of site that encourages the positive use of the Internet. The site encourages users to share one good thing via text or video as a counter to online bullying and trolling.

2. **Commonsensemedia.org** This is a site that is dedicated to educating and advocating for children and families. The site has a section called Parent Concerns that gives tips on everything from screen time to using technology as a learning resource. Specific to our topic, they also provide resources for social media and cell phone use.

3. **The Family Online Safety Institute** This is a sophisticated site that has a great section entitled Good Digital Parenting. This section provides tips in the form of videos and blogs to help you based on the age of your child. This site also provides a .pdf file of online safety cards. These cards are an amazing tool to use when giving your child a new piece of technology. The cards can function as the working agreement between you and your child for the use of the device. It is set up as an actual contract that the child signs. This way you both agree to the parameters you set but it also means that you will have to have discussions with your child about those limits and the risk in using the device.

4. **Ikeepsafe.org** This is an interesting site and accompanying app. The premise of this organization is to help families develop and prepare their children to be "ethical, responsible and resilient digital citizens." The app helps the family assess several areas of digital influence. These include: balance, ethics, privacy, reputation, relationships, and online security. I really like the idea of instilling sound digital use ethics into adolescents. This app provides a large amount of wonderful fuel for family discussions about technology use, not only about social networking but also about the other realms of digital use including being able to balance screen time with the rest of our lives.

5. **Staysafeonline.org** This is a site run by the National Cybersecurity Alliance. This site does not directly deal with cybersex or parenting but is a good resource for teaching online safety in a global sense. The information on this site includes identity theft, spam, phishing, etc. This is a great resource to get yourself up to date before you talk to your child about online risk.

6. **NetSmartz.org** This site is run by the National Center for Missing and Exploited Children. It has informational sections for parents, educators, law enforcement, teens and kids. In the parents section you can choose from many topics including: cell phones, children as victims, sexual content, sexting, cyberbullying and many more. If you click on the Inappropriate Content for Children section, the content provides tips for protecting children from sexual content. What I like best about this section of the site is that it not only provides tips but it also has a section for what it calls "Discussion Starters." They provide five questions that a parent can use to talk about the uncomfortable subject with their child. For these discussion topics specifically, please see the site link at http:// www.netsmartz.org/InappropriateContent.

7. **Safekids.com** This is another site by Larry Magid, who also created connectsafely.org. This site appears to be an adjunct to the main connectsafely.org site.

8. **Cyberwise.org** This is a content rich site that provides information for parents about technology. Their slogan is "No grownups left behind." In addition to safety information, this is another site that talks a lot about digital citizenship and cybercivics. This is not something that you hear the average person talking about. However, these are great conversations to have. What are the ethics of using social media, for example? This site also has a great social media presence, being very active on sites like twitter, which make it much more relevant for the parenting crowd that are more digital native than digital immigrant.

9. **Pornproofkids.org This is a site that provides some content in the form of blog posts.** However, it is not as information and tip heavy as many of the other sites. The main thing this site does is promote the great book, Good Pictures, Bad Pictures that I will talk about a bit later. This site's main premise is to keep kids from seeing pornography at all. I make no

judgment on this but want to let you know ahead of time. This may fit perfectly with some parenting models and not as well with others.

FILTERING AND MONITORING APPS AND SOFTWARE

First, I want to say that there is no way I will be able to provide you with an exhaustive list of every filtering and monitoring program out in the cyber universe. I will provide information on different types of filtering and the most commonly used software programs or apps. Again, my purpose here is not to promote one program over another but to provide you with information on the resources available.

Monitoring that Doesn't Invade a Child's Privacy

POCKETGUARDIAN

I first became aware of PocketGuardian last year (2015) when the app was in the development stages. I was immediately interested in it as the app provided something different then the options available at the time. Current options were very much along the lines of completely blocking your child's access to certain things or software that allows a parent to see every single thing a child does in the digital world.

Psychologically, I don't like the idea of a parent seeing every single text, email or social media post a child makes. I do feel that a child is entitled to some level of privacy. Filtering and blocking are imperfect and spying is intrusive. PocketGuardian provides another option.

At the time of this writing, I asked one of the founders to provide me with some information about the app and why they developed it. Jason France, one of the founders, very kindly replied with the following:

"PocketGuardian was developed by two dads with the goal of keeping kids safe online. After hearing numerous stories of kids taking their lives due to online harassment, they were driven to develop a means of alerting parents to inappropriate content while protecting their child's privacy. They don't envision PocketGuardian as a silver bullet to online harassment, but rather a tool parents can use to be made aware of their digital kids activities and help parents discuss online safety with their children.

PocketGuardian is the first parental monitoring service to keep parent's actively aware of their child's digital footprint without invading their privacy. Parents who use PocketGuardian receive alert notifications when inappropriate content is detected on their child's mobile device and social media accounts. Each notification identifies the type of inappropriate content, the mobile app or social media site where the content was detected, and whether the content was sent or received by the child. Notifications also include parental resources to help parents start a healthy conversation with their child. The inappropriate content itself is never included in order to protect the child's privacy, maintain parent-child trust, and save them from embarrassment."

PocketGuardian is so much more than a great story about two dads who were worried about their kids and took action. It is an app that figures respect and privacy into the equation. You can respect your child's privacy and still set limits and boundaries. I believe that removing the intrusiveness of other apps that spy goes a long way to help children trust parents. Part of why kids don't tell their parents about the inappropriate things they see online is that they are afraid that their parents will freak out. Another thing I like about this app is the removal of the embarrassment. Having a parent-child conversation about sex, sexting, pornography, bullying, etc., is difficult enough. It is even more difficult for the child when the parents are holding their phone, looking at the offending image, text or social media post. This app helps parents be aware of what their children are doing online. It facilitates communication. It respects privacy and it is not intrusive. I give it a huge thumbs up.

Free Traditional monitoring software and apps:

Before we start talking about external sources of monitoring that you have to pay for, let's talk about those controls already available, for free, on your current devices. Whether you are a MAC user or a PC user, the most up-to-date operating systems for each come with built in parental controls that you can employ.

For MAC, you can find the parental control options in the System Preferences (https://support.apple.com/kb/ph18571?locale=en_US). OS operating systems allow parents to do many things. You can specify what apps a child can access. A parent can also set limits on what apps the child can see, limiting them specifically or by age range. The parental controls allow you to limit access to certain websites. Another great feature that is available is the ability to restrict a child's contact with other people in the game center. One thing that many parents do not realize is that their child can talk to anyone in many of the Internet enabled games. Most have some sort of chat function. Apple allows you to limit your child's ability to do this. You can also use restrictions on email. The OS controls also allow a parent to limit the amount of time a child spends online. This may be a good option for younger children or children who are spending too much time online and not getting homework or other chores finished.

There are a few other things that the parental controls allow you to do but I want to talk specifically about the built in web camera. The parental controls allow you to turn off the built in web camera. Many parents don't think about their children using the webcam on the computer as much as they worry about the camera on a smartphone or tablet. As discussed earlier in the book, many of the youth produced sexual images are created on a webcam on a computer and not a phone. These images are often created when the child has the laptop or PC in their own room with a fully functioning built in camera. This is something that parents need to be aware of and for younger children it is highly recommended that you turn the camera off. If your child needs or wants to use the camera, they can come to you and ask for the control to be temporarily lifted.

The Apple iPhone also has some really good, built in, restrictions. We often use these with our clients who are trying to abstain from viewing pornography on their phone. You can go to general settings and enable certain restrictions. For my adult clients, we often restrict adult content, the use of the camera, and the ability to download and delete apps. One proviso for using restrictions on an iPhone that we have encountered: when the iPhone updates its operating system, sometimes the restrictions will need to be reset. Also, if you have a tech savvy teen, they may know how to reboot the system and get rid of the restrictions as well. The process is similar for an iPad.

When it comes to Microsoft Operating Systems, I know that many of us are using many different versions. The current, most recent version at the time of this writing is Windows 10. No matter what version of Windows you are using, or at least the more recent versions (7 and up, Vista), there are some level of parental controls. Windows 10 allows parents to monitor in multiple ways. One option available is for a parent to be able to view a child's web browsing activity and what apps they are using. This usage can be emailed to a parent in a weekly report. Windows allows you to block specific websites and apps that you know your child has previously visited. Based on the activity report, you can see the websites your child is using. You can click on them to check them out (or not if the name is quite explicit enough). From there, you can block your child's access to these websites. All of this can be done without your child's knowledge.

The weekly email reports are a helpful, quick way to see what your child is doing online. However, I would recommend that you talk to your child about any site you see that is questionable rather than simply locking it down without discussion. The ability to block a website remotely from an activity report allows both the parent and the child to hide from critical communication. If the parent shuts down a pornography site and doesn't talk to their child about it, the likelihood of the child coming to them to complain when they can no longer access the site is minimal.

In addition to the activity monitoring and blocking function, there are other parental controls available. A parent can block adult content. However, the ability to block this content is only functional on Microsoft based browsers. If you are going to do this, you also need to ensure that there are no other browsers on your computer and your child cannot download another browser. A savvy teenager will quickly learn what browsers he or she can and cannot use and will download another option. Therefore, you may get a sparkling clean activity report while your child is using an unmonitored browser to access inappropriate content.

These parental controls also allow you to always allow or always block specific websites. You can also set content age limits for apps and games with the OS parental controls as well as screen time limits. The screen time limits can be set to vary based on the day of the week or time of day. Another function of these parental controls is the ability to put parental controls on a child's X-box gaming system. Gaming systems are something that not all parents think about when monitoring their child's digital use. Having some limits for gaming can be helpful, especially for younger teens and children.

Each web browser that you use also has some level of filtering available. Depending on what browser you use, you can personalize your filtering of content. Any filtering that you put in place on a specific browser works only for that browser. You need to make sure either that there is only one browser option available on the computer or that you block the ability to download another browser. This can fall into the "where there is a will, there is a way category." A determined teenager will either figure out how to get around this or will simply download another browser to use.

Paid Traditional Monitoring Software and Apps

If you do not wish to use the operating system or browser controls (or you want to double filter), you can choose one of the many external filtering and monitoring software options. There are a large number of options available. Each brand has its own distinctive features. If you choose to purchase a monitoring or filtering software, there are several things you need to consider. Make sure you do your research. Are you an Apple person or a non-Apple person? Are you a mixed Apple person like me with an Android phone, a Windows based laptop and an iPad? This makes a difference. Not all software will work on both Apple and non-Apple devices. Before you start researching programs, make sure you truly understand what devices you want covered. Options include: computers, phones, tablets, gaming systems, and eReaders such as the Kindle. If you are going to use a filtering program, you need to think about it first and then do your research. If you are a mixed OS household, you may end up needing several programs which can complicate things.

Doing the Research: Best Reviewed Sites

There are many sites you can look at to help you in your research. I often go to the Top Ten Reviews site as I like how it breaks down and compares software. The most recent list was published in 2015, breaking down the top ten Parental Software programs of 2016 (http://parental-software-review.toptenreviews.

com/). The Net Nanny program received the highest rating in this review. Net Nanny (www.netnanny.com) is a very common program. This program received the highest rating for a number of reasons. It provides a high level of filtering including: website filtering and content, chat and messaging blocking, blocking of the ability to transfer files, social networking blocking, online search filtering, app blocking, gaming content filtering, and profanity masking. Of all the programs reviewed that landed in the top ten, Net Nanny was the only one that had a profanity blocker. Net Nanny also allows a parent to record various aspects of their child's digital life. If you use Net Nanny, you can record online searches, websites visited, email, social networking, usernames and passwords, and chat. It also has a remote reporting feature. One of the best things, in my opinion, for ease of use, is that Net Nanny is compatible with Android phones, iPhones, Mac OS, and four different versions of Windows operating systems. The review also stated that Net Nanny was easy to use and install and had good customer support.

Second on the top ten review list is the program, WebWatcher (www. webwatcher.com). This program has all of the same filtering and blocking options as Net Nanny but does not have a profanity blocker. It also has the same recording features as Net Nanny with the addition of screen shot play-back. If a program has screen shot capability, it will, at predetermined intervals, take and record screen shots of what is on the computer screen. This is actu-ally how the Federal government monitors the web activity of sex offenders (though not this program). If you use the screen shot option, you can literally see what imagery your child has seen online. Web Watcher is compatible with most devices except for the iPhone. Therefore, if you are a mixed computer household and you have devices with Windows software and someone has an iPhone, this software may not be for you.

Ranking number three on this list is McAfee's Safe Eyes program (www. internetsafety.com). This is a very commonly used monitoring program. I have many clients who use Safe Eyes (as well as Net Nanny). In terms of filtering and blocking capabilities, it is very similar to Net Nanny and Web Watcher. Safe Eyes also records the same things as the above two programs without screen shot capabilities. One of the nice things about Safe Eyes is that it comes with three licenses instead of one which means that three computers can run the software as opposed to just one license which is more common. Safe Eyes does have one compatibility issue. It works on iPhones as well as Mac OS and Windows

OS. However, it does not work on Android phones. Compatibility with Android phones is an issue with a number of monitoring software.

If you want details on the full top ten list, you can see the site listed above. The·other programs that landed in the top ten were: Witigo Parental Filter (www.witigo.com), Content Barrier (www.https://www.intego.com/contentbarrier) which is only for MAC, SpyTech Spy Agent (http://www.spytech-web.com/), Cybersitter (www.cybersitter.com), Verity (http://www.nchsoftware.com/child-monitoring/), and Elite Key Logger (http://www.elite-keylogger.net/). Personally, I do not like programs such as Key Logger that are spy software. From a psycho-logical perspective, outright spying is not the best way to form a relationship with your child that fosters open communication and safety.

There is no way that I can provide you a comprehensive list of very single program available that monitors or filters digital devices. Here are a few other programs that you can add to your list to research should you choose to go the filter route:

- *Norton Family - https://onlinefamily.norton.com/family-safety/features.fs*

- *K9 Web Protection - http://www1.k9webprotection.com/*

- *PhoneSherriff - http://www.phonesheriff.com/*

- *Qustodio - https://www.qustodio.com/en/*

- *MyMobileWatchdog - https://www.mymobilewatchdog.com/*

- *Covenant Eyes - http://www.covenanteyes.com/?promocode=techmission*

- *x3Watch - http://x3watch.com/?v=1.4*

- *Mobicip - http://www.mobicip.com/*

- *Content Protect - https://www.contentwatch.com/*

Again, this is not an exhaustive list of options, but a place to start your research into monitoring software.

DNS Filtering

Another option is to filter via DNS or Domain Name System. I confess that I am not as familiar with this option as others. I have a rather tech savvy client who was my entree into the DNS world. If you use this option, you will be filtering at the level of your router so all devices using your wi-fi will be covered.

The following is an explanation on DNS from one of my tech savvy clients (an anonymous thank you).

"OpenDNS is a solution for protecting all devices on a network. DNS is an initialism of Domain Name Server (or Service). When you type Google.com into your browser, DNS works behind the scenes to look up the server's numeric address, and then route your browser across the Internet to your destination.

Think of DNS like a GPS. Your house is at a specific latitude and longitude, but that's not what you give your friend when you invite them over to your house. You give your friend your address and they type that into their GPS. The GPS then routes them to that address using the longitude and latitude it associates with your address.

By using OpenDNS you can specify the route devices on your network take for different websites. If your child types Google.com into the browser, OpenDNS sends them to Google. But if they try to go somewhere off-limits, OpenDNS will change the destination to a safe page.

OpenDNS provides two solutions. OpenDNS Family Shield is the simplest option requiring no account and minimal setup. OpenDNS Home requires an account and more setup but provides more options such as statistics, logs, and blocking for a greater range of websites by category (i.e. social networks, blogs, classified ads, etc.).

Be aware of what OpenDNS can't do:

Any device that has unfettered access to network and security settings can easily be modified to bypass OpenDNS's servers. So, any device that isn't locked down to block access to device configuration is at risk.

OpenDNS can't stop traffic that isn't on your network. This includes phones or tablets that have cellular data service, and devices that are used on multiple Wi-Fi networks. i.e. connecting your child's tablet to Public Wi-Fi."

Some DNS options you may wish to consider:

- OpenDNS - https://www.opendns.com home-internet-security/
- SafeDNS - https://www.safedns.com/ safe-internet-at-home

Books and Other Helpful Resources

It is in any parent's best interests to get as educated as possible. I highly recommend reading as much as you can from reputable sources. Below you will find a reading list that may be helpful in learning how to talk to your child about sex and sexuality.

Good Pictures, Bad Pictures – This is a book published in 2014 by the organization, PornProofKids.com. The book is geared for smaller children and is meant to be a read along story with mom or dad.

How to Talk with Teens About Love, Relationships, and S-E-X by Amy G. Miron and Charles D. Miron

Sex & Sensibility: The Thinking Parent's Guide to Talking Sense About Sex by

Deborah M. Roffman

Sexuality: Your Sons and Daughters With Intellectual Disabilities by Karin

Melberg Schwier and David Hingsburger

Staying Connected to Your Teenager: How to Keep Them Talking to You and How to Hear What They're Really Saying by Michael Riera

Teaching Children with Down Syndrome about Their Bodies, Boundaries, and Sexuality by Terri Couwenhoven

The Real Truth About Teens and Sex: From Hooking Up to Friends with Benefits — What Teens Are Thinking, Doing, and Talking About, and How to Help Them Make Smart Choices by Sabrina Weill

Why Do They Act That Way?: A Survival Guide to the Adolescent Brain for You and Your Teen by David Walsh

Talk to Me First: Everything You Need to Know to Become Your Kids' "Go-To" Person about Sex by Deborah Roffman

For Goodness Sex: Changing the Way We Talk to Teens About Sexuality, Values, and Health by Al Vernacchio.

A newer entrance into the field of sexuality books for parents are three books called *30 days of Sex Talks* for Ages 12+, 8-11 and 3-7. These books offer discussion points for parents and are created by Educate and Empower Kids.

In addition to books on sex and sexuality, it is also helpful to learn more about the adolescent brain. My favorite book on the topic is *The Teenage Brain: A Neuroscientist's Survival Guide to Raising Adolescents and Young Adults*. This is a very well written book by noted researcher and author Dr. Francis Jensen. The book will give you a primer on adolescent brain development and share how the specifics of the adolescent brain affects all types of learning and behavior.

Another excellent book on the subject is *Brainstorm: The Power and Purpose of the Teenage Brain* by Daniel Siegel, M.D. This book also delves into brain science to help parents understand the workings of their teenager's mind. An excellent book on fostering communication between parents and children is *How to Talk so Kids Will Listen and Listen so Kids Will Talk* by Adele Faber and Elaine Mazlish.

Thus far, we have been discussing resources for monitoring a teen's digital use or for parental education. If, in your discussions with your teen, or through some other disclosure, you come to find that your teenage has a problem with online pornography, that it is interrupting his or her life functioning, you will need further resources as well. It is imperative that your child sees a therapist who is qualified and educated in working with issues of pornography addiction or sexual addiction and compulsivity. If your child has a general Internet addiction and not pornography or sexual related use, you also need to make sure that your child sees someone who specializes in Internet Addiction Counseling.

At present there are only two organizations that train and certify therapists to work with sexual addiction. Pornography addiction, chat issues, etc., can all fall under this broad moniker. The first is the International Institute for Trauma and Addiction Professionals (www.iitap.com). If a therapist completes this training, he or she will carry the credential of Certified Sex Addiction Therapist or CSAT. This is the credential that I have--and I have done further training to be a supervisor. In order to become a CSAT, a therapist has to commit to four full weeks of classroom training combined with supervised practice. In order to become certified a clinician needs to do at least 30 hours of supervision on the topic as well.

One of the things I like about IITAP's certification program is its rigorous nature. Taking on four full weeks of training over a period of time, plus over 30 hours of supervision, speaks to the level of commitment that CSAT's have in learning this work. Not everyone can work with sexual issues, and the rigorous nature of this training tends to weed out those therapists who really do not have a passion for the work. A CSAT trained therapist will be able to assess your child to first determine if he or she has a problem related to some form of compulsive sexuality. They may or may not have a problem but it is best to have a profes- sional assess them to make that determination. Many of the adolescents we see do not, in fact, have a pornography addiction, though some do. On the IITAP website (www.iitap.com) there is a "find a therapist" page that you can use to find a trained therapist near you.

The other organization that trains clinicians to work with sexual addic- tion issues (the broad moniker for compulsive sexuality like pornography) is the Society for Sexual Health (SASH). SASH has what they call Advanced Training for Problematic Sexual Behaviors, which is a certificate program. The Level 1 training for this certificate is not necessarily done in person but frequently done online or via video. There are 8 classes that a clinician takes. They then do an in-person training that is two days. This training does give a clinician a basic overview of the work. There is no supervision necessary for the credential and the training is much less in-depth than the IITAP certification process. The SASH website (www.sash.net) does have a section for you to find a therapist.

There is another therapeutic option available if you have questions relat- ing to your own or your child's sexuality, seeing a sex therapist. Without getting into the political infighting in the therapeutic community, I will simply say that sex therapists, for the most part, do not believe that sexual addiction or pornog- raphy addiction is real or exists. This is an ongoing argument in the therapeu- tic community that is outside the realm of this book. A sex therapist is a great resource for sexual education, learning about "out of the box" sexual interests and working through issues such as sexual dysfunction. I think that there is a role for sex therapists in this work as well. I have a sex therapist currently working as an intern in my sexual addiction therapy practice. She brings an alternative perspective to client issues that I welcome. That being said, if your child truly has a pornography addiction, a sex therapist may not be the best type of clinician to consult. Sex therapists are licensed by the American Association of Sexuality Educators, Counselors and Therapists. Their website (www.aasect.org) can help you find a sex therapist near you.

If your child has an Internet addiction, other treatment options are available. Internet addictions can include behaviors such as cybersex but also frequently involve gaming, chatting or social networking. Just like with sexual addiction, there are in-patient rehabilitation facilities for this problem. One of the first Internet Addiction treatment programs is the reSTART (www.netaddictionrecovery.com) program. ReSTART is a residential program in Washington State developed by Hilarie Cash and her colleagues and is one of the best programs in the country.

Another great resource to have for Internet Addiction is www.netaddiction.com. This site is run by Dr. Kimberly Young who is a pioneer in the field of Internet Addiction. This site provides a lot of great information for parents and you can, if you live near Philadelphia, PA, see her for counseling. Dr. Young also founded the Internet Addiction Program at the Bradford Regional Medical Center in Bradford, PA. This is a 10 day, hospital based recovery program for Internet Addiction.

If you are not sure what type of therapeutic help you or your child need, the best resource out there is the Psychology Today website (www.psychologytoday.com). On the Psychology Today website there is a find a therapist section. On this page, you simply enter your zip code and an extensive list of therapists in your area will appear. Nearly every single therapist, psychologist and psychiatrist I know has a listing on the *Psychology Today* website. Each therapist will have a profile on the page that will list their areas of specialty in practice. This will allow you to immediately know whether or not a therapist will be able to competently deal with your issue at hand.

There is no way to provide you with an exhaustive list of each and every resource available for monitoring, education or treatment. My goal in this chapter was to provide you with a place to start your information gathering. If you are a parent of a younger child, my suggestion is to start reading about healthy sexuality and how to talk to your child about sex. Younger children also do better with more strict digital monitoring. As your child gets older, and you continue the discussions and open communication, these restrictions can be decreased, changed or lifted. If you think, at any time, that your child's behavior may be problematic, don't wait to check it out. I would much rather see an adolescent for an assessment and happily tell the parent that their child's behavior is not problematic than have the parent wait until there is a crisis such as a school sexting scandal.

Final Thoughts

My original goal in writing this book was to have it serve as a tool for prevention. I love the work that I do to help my clients who are sex addicts. Every day is an adventure. Every day I am blessed with being part of the difficult recovery process of my clients, and I am blessed that I can walk along beside them for a part of their journey to wholeness.

With that being said, there is a long standing line of banter between me and my clients. I always tell them that I would be overjoyed if everyone in the world got healthy and didn't need to come to sex addiction therapy. I will go ride horses for a living. They inevitably reply, not to worry, you have job security. The problem is that I don't want job security. I have a rather optimistic streak (some may call it a fantasy) that suggests that we can decrease the number of problems in our children, who then become adults, if we improve parent-child communication and connection. The sex addicts I work with are longing for connection. They have attachment issues. These attachment issues stem from childhood and relationships with caregivers.

If only a handful of parents who read this book start to communicate with their child about sexuality in a healthy, non-shaming manner, I feel like it will have been worth the time and effort of writing. We need to start talking about sex in an open manner. It is not shameful but a natural mammalian behavior. If we can begin to openly discuss these issues, we begin to peel away the layers of shame associated with sex and sexuality. Shame is a key component of addiction. If there is less shame there is less addiction. If there is more healthy connection between parents and their children, there is less attachment related addiction. The world will then be, in some tiny measure, a healthier place.

References

As this book is not a scientific publication, but a parenting book, I did not cite the specific details of all of the research that was reviewed and talked about in this book. This was meant as no disrespect to the authors of said research studies nor the scientific journals in which they are published. Citing research in the traditional fashion required in journals is a bit cumbersome to read for the lay person who is not accustomed to filtering through numerous citations at the end of a sentence.

Below is a list of all of the scientific work that I read and/or included in this book. If you wish to read any of these yourself, the best option is to go to the library of your local college or university. Members of the general public can usually access these libraries and from there, you can access the digital journal archives. Personally, as I am no longer in academia, I am grateful to the library of Penn State Lehigh Valley campus. It has been many years since graduate school and camping out in front of the computer searching references brought with it a sense of nostalgia.

Thank you to the following authors and researchers for their fine work. Keep it coming.

Akre, C., Berchtold, A., Gmel, G., & Suris, J. (2014). The evolution of sexual dysfunction in young men aged 18-26 years. *Journal of Adolescent Health, in press.* 1-8.

Angelides, S. (2013). "Technology, hormones and stupidity": The affective politics of teenage sexting. *Sexualities, 16(5/6).* 665-689.

Baumgertner, S. E., Sumter, S. R., Peter, J., Valkenburg, P. M. & Livingstone, S. (2014). Does country context matter? Investigating the predictors of teen sexting across Europe. *Computers in Human Behavior, 34.* 157-164.

Bentosch, E. G., Snipes, D. J., Martin, A. M. & Bull, S. S. (2013). Sexting, substance abuse, and sexual risk behavior in young adults. *Journal of Adolescent Health, 52.* 307-313.

Beyens, I., Vandenbosch, L. & Eggermont, S. (2015). Early adolescent boys' exposure to internet pornography: Relationships to pubertal timing, sensation seeking, and academic performance. *Journal of Early Adolescence, 35(8).* 1045-1068.

Campbell, S. W. & Park. Y. J. (2014). Predictors of mobile sexting among teens: Toward a new explanatory framework. *Mobile Media and Communication, 2(1).* 20-39.

Cookingham, L. M. & Ryan, G. L. The impact of social media on the sexual and social wellness of adolescents, *Journal of Pediatric and Adolescent Gynecology* (2104), doi: 10.1016/j.jpag.2014.03.001.

Cyberbullying Research Center (2015). State sexting laws. Www.cyberbullying.us

Dir, A.L., Coskumpinar, A., & Cyders, M.A. A meta-analytic review of the relationship between adolescent risky sexual behavior and impulsivity and risky sexual behavior across gender, age and race, *Clinical Psychology Review* (2014), doi: 10.1016/j.cpr.2014.08.004

Doornwaard, S. M., Morena, M.A., van den Eijnden, R. J.J.M., Vanwesenbeeck, I., & ter Bogt, T. F. M. (2014). Young adolescent's sexual and romantic reference displays on Facebook. *Journal of Adolescent Health, 55.* 535-541.

Faccio, E., Iudici, A., Costa N. & Belloni, E. (2014). Cyberbullying and interventions programs in school and clinical setting. *Procedia- Social and Behavioral Sciences, 122.* 500-505.

Floros, G. & Siomos, K. (2013). The relationship between optimal parenting, internet addiction and motives for social networking in adolescence. *Psychiatry Research, 209.* 529-534.

Fortenberry, J.D. (2013). Puberty and adolescent sexuality. *Hormones and Behavior, 64.* 280-287.

Giedd, J. N. (2012). The digital revolution and adolescent brain development. *Journal of Adolescent Health, 51.* 101-105.

Gomez, L. C. & Ayala, E. S. (2014). Psychological aspects, attitudes and behaviour related to the practice of sexting: a systematic review of the existent literature. *Procedia- Social and Behavioral Sciences, 132.* 114-120.

Gordon-Messer, D., Bauermeister, J. A., Grodzinski, A., & Zimmerman, M. (2013). Sexting among young adults. *Journal of Adolescent Health, 52.* 301-306.

Greenfield, P. M. (2004). Inadvertent exposure to pornography on the Internet: Implications of peer-to-peer file-sharing networks for child development and families. *Applied Developmental Psychology, 25.* 741-750.

Hoffman, B. (2014). Computer as a threat or an opportunity for development of children. *Procedia – Social and Behavioral Sciences, 146.* 15-21.

Jia, H., Wisniewski, P., Xu, H., Rosson, M .B., & Carroll, J. M. (2015). Risk-taking as a learning process for shaping teen's online information privacy behaviors. *CSCW '15, March 14-18, 2015, Vancouver, BC, Canada.*

Jonsson, L.S., Priebe, G., Bladh, M. & Svedin, C. G. (2014). Voluntary sexual exposure online among Swedish youth- social background, internet behavior and psychosocial health. *Computers in Human Behavior, 30.* 181-190.

Kaljee, L. M., Green, M., Lerdboon, P., Riel, R., Pham. V., Tho, L.H., Ha, N.T., Minh, T. T., Li, X., Chen, X., & Stanton, B. (2011). Parent-youth communication and concordance between parents and adolescents on reported engagement in social relationships and sexually intimate behaviors in Hanoi and Khanh Hoa Province, Vietnam. *Journal of Adolescent Health, 48.* 268-274.

Karaian, L. (2012). Lolita speaks: "Sexting," teenage girls and the law. *Crime, Media, Culture, 8*(1). 57-73.

Klettke, B., Hallford, D. J., & Mellor, D. J. (2014). Sexting prevalence and correlates: A systematic literature review. *Clinical Psychology Review, 34.* 44-53.

Kopecky, K. (2016). Misuse of web cameras to manipulate children within the so-called webcam trolling. *Telematics and Informatics, 33.* 1-7.

Levine, D. (2013). Sexting: A terrifying health risk....or the new normal for young adults? *Journal of Adolescent Health, 52.* 257-258.

Lievens, E. (2014). Bullying and sexting in social networks: Protecting minors from criminal acts or empowering minors to cope with risky behaviour? *International Journal of Law, Crime and Justice, 42.* 251-270.

Lippman, J. R. & Campbell, S. W. (2014). Damned if you do, damned if you don't...if you're a girl: relational and normative contexts of adolescent sexting in the United States. *Journal of Children and Media, published online: 06 Jun 2014.*

Livingstone, S. & Gorzig, A. (2014). When adolescents receive sexual messages on the internet: Explaining experiences of risk and harm. *Computers in Human Behavior, 33.* 8-15.

Livingstone, S., Kirwil, L., Ponte, C. & Staksrud, E. (2014). In their own words: What b others children online? *European Journal of Communication, 29*(3). 271-288.

Ma, C.& Shek, D. T. L., (2013). Consumption of pornographic materials in early adolescents in Hong Kong. *Journal of Pediatric and Adolescent Gynecology, 26.* 518-525.

Madden, M., Cortesi, S., Grasser, U., Lenhart, A., & Duggan, M. (2012). Parents, teens, and online privacy. Pew Research Center, www.pewinternet.org/Reports/2012/Teens-and-Privacy.Aspx.

Madden, M., Lenhart, A., Cortesi, S., Grasser, U., Duggan, M., Smith, A., & Beaton, M. (2013). Teens, social media, and privacy. Pew Resarch Center, www.pewinterent.org/Reports/2013/Teens-Social-Media-And-Privacy.aspx.

Malamuth, N. & Huppin, M. (2005). Pornography and teenagers: The importance of individual differences. *Adolescent Medicine, 16.* 315-326.

McCabe, K. A., & Johnston, O. C. (2014). Perception on the legality of sexting: A report. *Social Science Computer Review, published online 24 March 2014.*

Mesch, G. S. (2009). Social bonds and internet pornographic exposure among adolescents. *Journal of Adolescence, 32.* 601-618.

Mitchell, K. J., Wolak, J., & Finkelhor, D. (2007). Trends in youth reports of sexual solicitation, harassment and unwanted exposure to pornography on the internet *Journal of Adolescent Health, 40*. 116-126.

Moreno, M. A. & Kolb, J. (2012). Social networking sites and adolescent health. *Pediatric Clinics of North America, 59*. 601-612

Morey, J. N., Gentzler, A. L., Creasy, B., Oberhauser, A. M. & Westerman, D. (2013). Young adults' use of communication technology within their romantic relationships and associations with attachment style. *Computers in Human Behavior, 29*. 1771-1778.

Nack, A. (2013). Film Review: Sext up Kids: How children are becoming hypersexualized. *Humanity and Society, 37*(3). 259-261.

Owens, E. W., Behun, R. J., Manning, J .C., & Reid, R. C. (2012). The impact of pornography on adolescents: A review of the research. *Sexual Addiction and Compulsivity, 19*. 99-122.

Padilla-Walker, L. M., Coyne, S. M., Fraser, A. M., Dyer, W. J. & Yorgason, J. B. (2012). Parents and adolescents growing up in the digital age: Latent growth curve analysis of proactive media monitoring. *Journal of Adolescence, 35*. 1153-1165.

Prensky, M. (2001). Digital natives, Digital Immigrants. *On the Horizon, 9*(5). 1-14.

Ringrose, J., Harvey, L., Gill, R. & Livingstone, S. (2013). Teen girls, sexual double standards and "sexting": Gendered value in digital image exchange. *Feminist Theory, 14*(3). 305-323.

Rosner, F., Gill, R. T., & Kohno, T. (2014). Sex, lies, or kittens? Investigating the use of Snapchat's self-destructing messages. *Financial Cryptography and Data Security, 8437*. 64-76.

Simpson, B. (2013). Challenging childhood, challenging children: Children's rights and sexting. *Sexualities, 16*(5/6). 690-709.

Soriano-Ayala, E., & Gonzalez-Jimenez, A. J. (2014). Spanish and Moroccan youths on social networks: A quantitative study in Spain. *Procedia-Social and Behavioral Sciences, 132*. 32-36.

Strasburger, V., Jordan, A.B., & Donnerstein, E. (2012). Children, adolescents, and the media; Health effects. *Pediatric Clinics of North America, 59*. 533-587.

Svedin, C. G., Akerman, I. & Priebe, G. (2011). Frequent users of pornography. A population based epidemiological study of Swedish male adolescents. *Journal of Adolescence, 34.* 779-788.

Temple, J. R., Le V. D., van den Berg, P., Ling, Y., Paul, J. A. & Temple, B. W. (2014). Brief report: Teen sexting and psychosocial health. *Journal of Adolescent Health, 37.* 33-36.

To, S., Sek-yum, S. & Iu Kan, S. (2012). Direct and mediating effects of accessing sexually explicit online materials on Hong Kong adolescents' attitude, knowledge, and behavior relating to sex. *Children and Youth Services Review, 34.* 2156- 2163.

Valcke, M., De Wever, B., Van Keer, H., & Schellens, T. (2011). Long-term study of safe use of young chlidren. *Computers and Education, 57.* 1292-1305.

Van Ouytsel, J., Walrave, M., Ponnet, K., & Heirman, W. (2015). The association between sexting, psychosocial difficulties, and risk behavior: Integrative Review. *The Journal of School Nursing, 31*(1). 54-69.

Walker, S., Sanci, L., & Temple-Smith, M. (2013). Sexting: Young women's and men's views on its nature and origins. *Journal of Adolescent Health, 52.* 697-701.

Wisniewski, P., Xu, H., Carroll, J. M. & Rosson, M. B. (2013). Grand challenges of researching adolescent online safety: A family systems approach. Proceedings of the Nineteenth Americas Conference on Information Systems, Chicago, Illinois, August 15-17, 2013. pp 1-8.

Wisniewski, P., Jia, H., Xu, H., Rosson, M.B., & Carroll, J. M. (2015). "Preventative" vs. "Reactive:" How parental mediation influences teens social media privacy behaviors. CSCW 2015. (Provided by author).

Wisniewski, P., Jia, H., Wang, N., Zheng, S., Xu, H., Rosson, M. B. & Carroll, J. B. (2015). Resilience mitigates the negative effects of adolescent internet addiction and online risk exposure. *CHI 2015, April 18-23, 2015, Seoul, Republic of Korea.*

Wolfe, S. E., Marcum, C. D., Higgins, G. E. & Ricketts, M. L. (2014). Routine cell phone activity and exposure to sext messages: Extending the generality of routine activity theory and exploring the etiology of a risky teenage behavior. *Crime & Delinquency, published online 15, July, 2014.* 1-31.

Wright, P.J. & Randall, A. K. (2012). Internet pornography exposure and risky sexual behavior among adult males in the United States. *Computers in Human Behavior, 28.* 1410-1416.

Ybarra, M. L., & Mitchell, K.J. (2005). Exposure to internet pornography among children and adolescents: A national survey. *CyberPsychology & Behavior, 8(5).* 473- 486.

Zillman, D. (2000). Influence of unrestrained access to erotica on adolescents' and young adults' dispositions toward sexuality. *Journal of Adolescent Health, 275.* 41-44.